11-7-85

# FANCY WATERFOWL

# OTHER TITLES AVAILABLE

*Domesticated Ducks and Geese*
Dr. J. Batty

*Pheasants of the World*
Dr. Jean Delacour

*The Budgerigar Book*
Ernest Howson

*Lizard Canaries and Other Rare Breeds*
G. T. Dodwell

*Hummingbirds*
A. J. Mobbs

# FANCY
# WATERFOWL

by
**Frank Finn**

**With coloured plates by**
**Frances Fry**

Distributor:
**NIMROD BOOK SERVICES**
PO Box 1,
Liss, Hants, GU33 7PR
England

ISBN 0 947647-08-2

Publisher:
**NIMROD BOOK SERVICES**
**(Fanciers Supplies Ltd)**
PO Box 1
Liss, Hants, GU33 7PR

Printed in England by S & R Printers, 236 Balham High Street, London SW17 7AW.

# CONTENTS

*Chapter*                                                          *Page*

Preface and Foreword . . . . . . . . . . .

Illustrations List . . . . . . . . . . . . . . .          vi

1   Management . . . . . . . . . . . . . . . .          1

2   Breeding, Hatching, and Rearing . . . . . .          11

3   Swans . . . . . . . . . . . . . . . . . . . . .          18

4   The True Geese . . . . . . . . . . . . . . .          22

5   Cereopsis, Magellan, and Egyptian Geese .          28

6   Shelducks . . . . . . . . . . . . . . . . . .          33

7   Muscovy, Mandarin, and Carolina Ducks .          38

8   Whistlers (Tree Ducks) . . . . . . . . . . .          46

9   The Mallard and its Allies . . . . . . . . .          51

10   Gadwall, Widgeons, and Shovellers . . . .          60

11   Teal . . . . . . . . . . . . . . . . . . . . .          64

12   Further Illustrations of Waterfowl . . . . . .          75

# FANCY WATERFOWL

## PREFACE

In writing the following brief account of the most popular fancy Waterfowl, I have endeavoured to give such description and details as may enable anyone who becomes interested in these beautiful birds to recognise such species as he will see in collections on ornamental waters, like that in St. James's Park, or find on sale with breeders and to treat them successfully if he decides to take up the Fancy on his own account.

I have confined myself to well known species only, but it must always be understood that, with the duck family as with other birds, even the familiar Finches, numerous charming species exist which only await the enterprise of someone who will put them on the market, a fact which has much impressed itself upon me during my residence in India, where so many of these birds can be easily obtained during the winter months, when European travellers commonly visit the country. I hope, however, that what I have written may be of interest to those who are interested in ornamental waterfowl.

F. FINN.

## EDITOR'S FOREWORD

In reissuing this book we are mindful of many changes which have taken place since the first edition. Nevertheless, there is clearly a text required which covers the subject in a clear and concise manner and for this reason the book has been republished suitably expanded to cover recent trends. Only the most popular species have been covered.

## LIST OF ILLUSTRATIONS

*Figure*                                                    *Page*

1.1   Fibre-glass pond suitably landscaped . . . . . . . . .   4

1.2   Spotted Bill Duck  . . . . . . . . . . . . . . . . .  10

2.1   Brooding by Infra-red lamp  . . . . . . . . . . .  13

3.1   Swans (a) Whooper
          (b) Bewicks
          (c) Mute  . . . . . . . . . . . . . . . .  20

4.1   Brent and Barnacle Geese . . . . . . . . . . . .  25

5.1   Magellan Geese  . . . . . . . . . . . . . . . . .  29

5.2   Ruddy Sheldrake . . . . . . . . . . . . . . . . .  32

7.1   Mandarin Drake and Duck . . . . . . . . . . . . .  41

8.1   Red-Billed Whistling Duck . . . . . . . . . . . .  49

11.1  Garganey . . . . . . . . . . . . . . . . . . . .  66

11.2  Red Crested Pochard . . . . . . . . . . . . . . .  73

# CHAPTER 1

## MANAGEMENT

Considering their obvious popularity in such places of public resort as the London parks, it is remarkable that ornamental waterfowl are not more kept by private fanciers in England. Were it generally known, also, that of all birds the duck tribe are about the easiest to keep and breed, even in a small space, and that they fetch good prices, the fancy for these beautiful creatures would be far more extensive than it is; even now many varieties appear in the show-pen, and some of the most striking await introduction to the public. But I propose at present to deal only with well-known and easily-obtained species, and what I have to say will, I hope, specially interest people who are fond of a few feathered pets, but can only spare a few minutes daily to attend to them, and to whom, very likely, a bird which can be allowed to run without damage in the cherished garden-plot is of more value than a champion who goes the rounds to win honours in the show-pen. To such as these the members of the duck family can be warmly commended; no birds require less attention, and there are none whose presence is less prejudicial to the gardener's hobby.

## PONDS AND ENCLOSURES

All ornamental ducks and geese of course require a pond; but on account of the small size of many of the former, and the terrestrial habits of the latter, the extent of water needed is in many cases very small, only, of course, provision must be made for keeping the water fresh and clean by having the pond cemented and fitted with a drain by which it can be emptied whenever it gets foul. The edges of the pond should be faced with brick or cement, to prevent the birds dabbling them away, if the water space is larger; and they should also be sloped, at any rate in places, to allow of the easy entrance and egress of the birds.

1

**Types of pond**

The enclosure surrounding the pond should be laid down, if possible, with grass, and in any case well planted with shrubs to afford shelter against sun and cold winds, and cosy nesting-sites as well; though nest-boxes like small dog-kennels should also be placed in convenient spots. Most waterfowl are very hardy, and need nothing else in the way of shelter from the weather.

The most important part, almost, of the enclosure is the fence surrounding it, which should be high enough to keep foxes and other predators out, and not too far from the water, so that the birds cannot stray too far away from it. If the space available is comparatively small, such as the end of a garden, for instance, I should strongly advise netting in the whole of it overhead, and leaving the birds unpinioned. Very coarse netting will do, and one has the consolation of knowing that one's pets are perfectly safe from cats at all events. Rats are not likely to damage old birds, except very small ones, such as Teal, and special means must be taken for protecting the ducklings.

Ponds vary from the very small miniature receptacle to an enormous water-filled area such as a miniature lake — usually a natural pond. Most waterfowl fanciers will have to be content with a small pond which is economical to maintain.

If a natural pond is available this usually fills and drains itself and this is a considerable advantage. On the other hand, the small artificial pond will require regular cleaning out and refilling. Fortunately, with a hose pipe the cleaning process is fairly simple. If some form of plug and draining pipe is incorporated into the design, all the better.

Possible types of pond are as follows:

1. **Ready-formed Ponds**
These may vary from old sinks, galvanized baths or fibreglass ponds purchased from a pet or aquarium shop. Each of these is cheap, but care must be taken to camouflage sinks or other modified vessels. This is usually done by sinking the "pond" well into the ground and covering the perimeter with flag-stones.

The pre-formed fibre-glass pond is a cheap and effective method of giving ducks a small area in which they can swim. A hole is excavated of the correct size and depth and the fibre-glass

2

container is placed into it. At first the hole may not be exactly correct and, therefore, by trial and error the exact fit should be obtained.

## 2. Ponds made with Liners

A suitable sized area is excavated and then is made "leak proof" by lining with a suitable material. This may be one of the following:

(a) **Polythene**

(b) **P.V.C.** (poly-vinyl-chloride) suitably reinforced

(c) **Butyl**

## 3. Concrete Ponds

A concrete pond, properly constructed, will probably outlast the other types. Obviously, though, it will take longer to make and may be more expensive.

There are a number of stages (after the hole is dug):

(a) Build up a layer of concrete 3-4 inches thick using a stiff mixture.

(b) Once the first layer is dried put on a further 3 inches, if necessary using battens to keep back the concrete to form the walls. Before dry, criss-cross the concrete.

(c) Finish off with smooth concrete to which has been added a waterproofing agent.

The normal concrete should be made up of ballast (3 parts), sharp sand (2) and cement (1); whereas the final mixture would be clean sharp sand (3) plus 1 part cement and, of course, the specified amount of waterproofing agent given in the manufacturer's instructions.

The final coat (the rendering) should be completed as quickly as possible to give a smooth finish and then allowed to dry slowly. In warm weather a covering of sacks or large paper bags might be advisable thus slowing down the drying process. Allow at least a complete week for the concrete to set and then fill with water and allow to stand for a period before allowing ducks to use the pond.

*Figure 1-1*  Fibre-glass Pond suitably landscaped

4

However, there are some experts who suggest that the pond should be scrubbed and emptied and then refilled a few times before allowing any livestock to enter the water. Certainly fish and water creatures — so essential to make a pond interesting — would have difficulty in surviving with a high level of lime in the water (from the concrete). This is why changing the water a number of times is advisable.

Cultivating weeds or other plants around a pond makes the water area more attractive. If space is available a complete water garden can be made with a combination of small ponds, shrubs, garden ornaments and grass. This can look very attractive and adds to the beauty of any garden, with the ducks being a positive asset. The important point to watch is not to overstock or the water garden may become muddy and unsightly.

If reeds are to be planted it will be necessary to have "islands" of clayey soil at the edge of the pond into which the roots can be placed. Stones placed in appropriate positions will help to prevent the soil being washed to the bottom of the pond.

When a large natural pond is available a small island in the centre may be used as a refuge for the ducks against predators. Indeed, when left out on a night, this will be essential; otherwise the fox will quickly kill all the ducks.

Fancy waterfowl do not take to duck houses as do the normal domesticated ducks.

## WATER SUPPLY

An adequate water supply is vital. This may be supplied by a hosepipe augmented by rain — in appropriate circumstances rain water can be drained from the house roof and channelled into the pond. Where a pond is small and there are no means of draining, the hose should be allowed to run for a long period to allow the existing water to be cleared. Usually this means allowing the water to overflow for a period until the foul, stagnant water has cleared.

When a river is available this may be used to fill a pond and, through a suitable outlet, the water can be allowed to run back into the river. The positioning of the pond must be done with great care thus enabling the water to flow naturally round a loop which leads through the pond.

If a river pond is possible, precautions will be necessary to make sure that the ducks do not stray on to the river and be carried away with the current or simply stray. A wire netting fence may be essential to avoid losses.

## Island shelter

I may here mention that any artificial pond in which ducks are kept, if too large to be entirely netted over, should have an island in the middle on which they might roost at night. They are quite intelligent enough to take advantage of this, and if a solid one cannot be made a raft will serve the purpose equally well. Rockwork is not needed as an adjunct to a duck-pond, as ducks are not usually rock-frequenting birds; but where any of the perching species are kept under cover unpinioned, dead branches should be fastened up for perches, and the nest-boxes hung high up, as such species also nest in trees. If pinioned birds are allowed to perch, the perches should project over the water, so that they can alight in this when leaving their roosts.

### PINIONING

If the birds are to be kept in open enclosures, or allowed their liberty on a large pond where they cannot readily be caught up, they must be pinioned. To do this, first find the joint in the wing which lies close in front of the knuckle or pinion-joint, nearer the tip of the wing; it is stiff and little moveable, and overhung by the little plume of feathers known as the bastard wing. This joint should be cut through with a sharp knife, and about five quills will be found to be severed from the wing thereby; the bleeding should be stopped with caustic.

Pinioning, although the birds do not mind it much, is not a nice operation to have to perform, and generally disfigures the bird a little, as if the wing is at all long the absence of the longest quills on one side gives a lop-sided appearance. I therefore do not advise it where the space given to the birds can be covered in; and I do not see that in the case of show birds it is needed at all, for if a bird can be caught for show it can be caught to have a wing cut. This operation need only be performed once a year, for ducks, unlike most other birds, drop all their quills at once, and renew them simultaneously, so that one clipping serves till the next moult.

# CHOOSING STOCK

Care should be taken, in the case of swans, geese, and larger ducks, not to keep more than a pair in the same enclosure if space is limited, and not to associate even other species with them without great care, as these birds are often very savage. Even with the smaller ducks, breeding pairs to be kept in the same enclosure should be of different species if breeding is desired. Of course if you merely want a pretty show, it is best to stick to drakes entirely, except where the sexes are both gaily coloured, as the homely plumage of the ducks, in my opinion, very much mars the effect of a mixed collection of both sexes. Unfortunately, in almost every case where the drake differs strikingly from the duck he assumes a plumage very closely resembling hers after she has gone to nest, and thus puts himself out of court as a show bird. Ducklings of both sexes in first feather are usually very like the old duck, but may have a special plumage of their own.

Ducks hybridise in confinement, and even in a wild state, with remarkable readiness, and the hybrids are sometimes very handsome, and not infrequently more or less fertile, though the various species of the duck tribe are as distinct as any others. This must be borne in mind by the breeder who wishes to keep his stock pure, and hybrids are best removed from the collection.

Where there is danger from rats, or where the parent birds are valuable, the eggs should be removed as soon as the duck has laid her full clutch and begun to sit, and hatched under a steady light hen. Some breeders very wisely recommend that the duck herself be given some eggs of the common wild duck by way of gratifying her natural maternal instincts. They also recommend that the eggs of fancy ducks, when incubated by a hen, should be covered by a piece of light woollen stuff when she is absent, as ducks are in the habit of covering their eggs with down at such times.

## FEEDING

The young ducklings can be fed on egg and breadcrumbs, and allowed plenty of duckweed, or, in the absence of that, lettuce or grass chopped up; later on small seeds and a little boiled minced liver may be given, and when the feathers are being assumed, grain should by degrees be added, and will ultimately be the sole food that need be given to the adult birds. Any ordinary poultry mixture will do, and it should be supplied in pans of water, so that the birds may eat it more comfortably, and that it may not be stolen by sparrows. Of course if the birds have the range of a large pond, one meal a day will be enough, except in time of frost, when, as in confinement, a larger quantity may be given. Indeed, with captive ducks grain may be left constantly with them. It is desirable also to allow confined birds plenty of duckweed whenever possible, and also water snails, which are much relished. They will also graze on the turf in their enclosure, which should be kept up by renewing it when necessary, as grass is not only useful as food, but more pleasant for the birds' feet than the bare ground. It is most unnatural for ducks to have to walk about on bare hard earth, and a hard floor should be avoided; if for any reason they have to be penned up, a layer of moss litter, dead leaves, etc., should be provided for them.

**Modern foodstuffs**

Although fancy waterfowl do not require specially formulated food this certainly helps when breeding (fertility and rearing improved). Possibilities are as follows:

1. **Starters** — usually turkey starter crumbs or chick crumbs.

2. **Growers** — turkey, broilers or poultry growers' pellets or mash.

3. **Breeders** — layers' pellets or mash.

Along with food and water ducks also require grit — this is particularly important when breeders are being kept. Under normal circumstances this will be taken by the birds quite naturally as they feed but when space is limited grit should be supplied.

## DISEASES

I have said nothing about ducks in disease, assuming that the intending duck fancier will be careful to buy only birds which appear active and in fairly good feather. If such be treated fairly, according to the directions I have laid down, they are not at all likely to fall ill, no birds enjoying better health than the ducks; while, if they do become diseased, they are not easy to treat.

I may, however, perhaps be permitted to mention here two causes of possible disaster, which I should have alluded to in the introduction, though no one who is observant of and thoughtful for his birds is likely to suffer thereby. One is the liability of ducks, when placed in a cage or other very confined space, to flutter wildly at nightfall, and hence injure themselves; and the other consists in the fact that the plumage of these birds, after they have been even for a few days debarred from bathing, loses its water-resisting properties and allows them to become thoroughly draggled when they do get a wash, so that chills or even drowning are likely to ensue. The remedies, or preventatives, are obvious; pens for ducks should have upright bars so as to afford no hold for the birds' feet, and should not be higher than they require to stand fully upright in; and when they are allowed access to a bath after long deprivation of it, they should not be allowed to stay in very long until the plumage has recovered its normal tone. Except in these two ways it is hardly possible to go wrong with ducks, which are generally blessed with excellent constitutions and tempers.

## SHOWING

In preparing ducks for show the chief thing is to over-come their natural timidity and aversion to close confinement, and herein lies one advantage in having them to hand in comparatively small enclosures, where they can be tamed and petted. Anyone who thinks of going in for the duck fancy should, if possible, pay a visit to the London Zoological Gardens, where these birds have for many years been very successfully kept.

The smallest members of the Duck family will, of course, interest a larger number of fanciers than the more cumbrous geese and swans, but since these are also much kept, and are intimately allied to the true ducks, I shall deal with the best known and most popular species of these also. But I do not recommend anyone to keep these birds who cannot give them a free range, as they are not suited for close captivity. How often one sees a pair of swans on an absurdly small piece of water, looking like the proverbial elephant in a dog-kennel. Half-a-dozen pairs of fancy ducks in the same space would be far more interesting and in keeping with their surroundings, and the additional outlay in fencing, etc., needed to protect them against vermin, which would not be dangerous to the larger birds, would be repaid by the superior value of the young obtained from them.

## CHAPTER 2

## BREEDING,

## HATCHING AND REARING

### BREEDING DUCKS

Generally speaking, ducks are easier to breed than large fowl or bantams and are less trouble to rear. Ducks are hardy creatures and from about 10 days old, provided the weather is reasonable, they are able to fend for themselves. However, in winter or early spring when heavy frosts occur some form of heat may be necessary up to 28 days old. This will be the case at night when the temperature falls to around freezing point.

### HATCHING

Hatching must take place when the ducks lay their eggs. Usually this is the Spring when the ducklings will "grow into" the better weather.

Many varieties of ducks do not come broody and therefore it will be necessary to use broody hens or an incubator (see later section on incubation). On the other hand, the ducks may be left to hatch their own eggs. Eggs may be maximised by removing eggs from the nests – usually after four have been laid.

For early hatched ducklings it will be necessary to use an incubator for the simple reason that broody hens are not generally available out of season.

Eggs should be collected daily and marked with the date. Around 12 eggs will be adequate for a setting. Settle the hen in a suitable box or coop on dummy eggs and after 1-2 days when she is sitting tight put the hatching eggs under her.

Take time and patience to settle the broody hens or many eggs will be lost. Remember a hen becomes attached to the nest in which she lays her eggs and in which she resolves to hatch them. A move to a different shed, where she can be in private, will most likely upset her so that she will not settle.

Try moving her after dark when she cannot see what is happening. Settle her down in the dark and then check the next day. If there is only one hen then confinement in a small shed in an open box will be fine. Leave water in a jar and mixed poultry corn in a container. The hen can then leave the nest at her own free will and return. If she does not leave, then after 48 hours remove her and let her run around and feed for around 10 minutes. Left too long some broodies will sit for excessively long periods and, without food and water, may die.

Where two or more broodies are to be used have a separate coop with a door for each. In this way control can be exercised by letting out one at a time until they have been trained to return to their own nest. After 2 or 3 days a few at a time may be allowed to exercise. However, this method is very time consuming and unless care is taken a hen may finish up on the wrong nest. Sometimes two hens will insist on returning to the same nest with unfortunate results.

A free-for-all, where broodies are allowed to sit where they will, does not produce good hatching results. Preferably a broody hen should have privacy in a quiet place, where she can sit in peace and, when necessary, have exercise, food and water. Failure to provide the correct environment and attention will lead to indifferent hatches and disappointments.

The sitting box should be filled with damp soil, shaped into a large "basin" and lined with straw or hay.

For good hatching results feed a layers' or breeders' ration. This may be obtained from the animal feeding mills in the form of mash or pellets; the latter are cleaner and there is less waste. Do not overfeed or the ducks will become too fat.

If exhibition birds are to be produced then top quality stock is essential. Establish the *standard* for the particular variety and then match the drake and ducks so that the "points of excellence" are brought out to the full on any progeny bred. The precise selection cannot be predetermined with certainty; this is why breeding winners is so difficult and yet so fascinating.

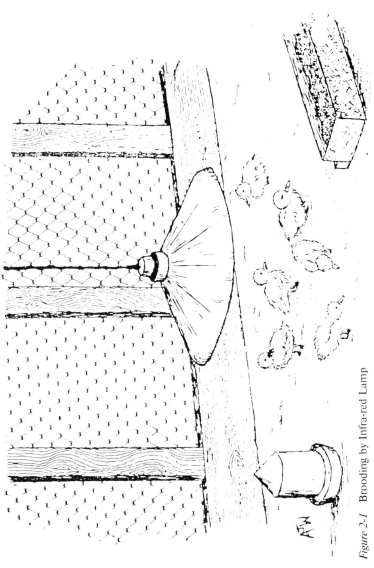

*Figure 2-1* Brooding by Infra-red Lamp

**Collecting Eggs**

Essential rules to follow with eggs are as follows:

1. Collect eggs early in the morning and clean off any mud. Some writers state that eggs should not be washed, but it has been shown that the hatch improves when a mild disinfectant is used to sterilize the eggs. This implies that eggs must be washed in some way. Note: Some birds may desert the nest if taken too early — from fourth egg may be safer.

2. Keep eggs for not longer than 7 days in a cool temperature (10-15⁰ C, 50-59⁰ F).

3. When the eggs are set, put the date on the small end of the egg or, in large incubators, put the date on a label in the tray.

4. Turn eggs regularly both when being stored and in the incubator. At least twice a day is essential.

## BROODING

Waterfowl may be reared by infra-red lamp, an oil lamp or a calor gas brooder. A small shed with the source of heat fitted is all that is necessary. The birds can be allowed to run on grass after a few days, but should be watched very carefully or crows, rats or other predators will take them. A covered run may be safer for a few weeks.

If reared by a broody hen, then a coop and enclosed run will be essential. This should be placed on grass and moved daily so that fresh grass is available. There should be a regular supply of water and, for the first few weeks, a regular supply of Turkey Starter Crumbs followed by other food.

In the early stages nourishing food is essential; grass alone will be inadequate for building up the waterfowl to the required size.

The water and food should be supplied from the second day and should be put in the run, under the protection of a door or board placed on top of the pen. Supply shavings in the bottom of the coop so that the hen and her brood are in dry surroundings and, of course, clean out and replace the shavings every few days.

*Drowning a danger*

Young ducklings and goslings, not allowed to go on to a pond for some time, may have difficulty is coping with swimming. Their plumage may not contain sufficient oils to avoid saturation and, therefore, they may have difficulty or even drown.

Introduce them to shallow water and watch for a few days to make sure that they are coping.

## ARTIFICIAL INCUBATION

Hatching the eggs of ducks or geese by incubator can be very difficult. At one time the success rate was extremely low. In recent years, with the improvement in incubators and in techniques, very good results have been obtained, but for the amateur there is obviously a great deal of care and patience required.

The main requirements are:

1. Correct temperature without too much fluctuation.

2. Correct level of humidity — vital for any type of waterfowl eggs.

**In all cases the instructions issued by the manufacturer of the incubator being used should be followed.** Moreover, it should be appreciated that the incubation principles vary according to the type of machine being employed so *general* rules are difficult to formulate. For example, a machine which incorporates a fan for ventilation and diffusing the heat, is quite a different proposition from one which relies on the air rising by itself.

## TYPES OF INCUBATOR

Broadly speaking incubators fall into two main categories:

1. **Still-air Incubators**
   These are usually small machines which hold from 25 to 300 hen eggs and obviously fewer duck or goose eggs. The heat is often over the eggs and there are ventilation holes at the bottom which allow the air to rise through the machine going through an outlet at the top.

Moisture for humidity is usually provided in a container at the base of the machine and should be filled, say, once each week.

2. **Forced-draught Incubators**
   These incorporate a fan and heating elements which bring the temperature to the appropriate level (usually around 99$^0$ F, 37.2$^0$ C). Both small and large machines incorporate this principle, although the fan does make a machine more expensive and for this reason is often provided in the larger machines only.

*Turning*
The smaller machines usually require turning to be done at least twice daily by hand. On the other hand, the large machines, having special loading trays into which the eggs are packed, allow eggs to be "turned" by moving the position of the trays. This may be done by the manual operation of a lever to move the trays or they may be turned quite automatically by electric motor.

Some of the more advanced smaller incubators incorporate automatic turning. Others use turning rings which allow the eggs to be turned by a simple movement of the rings.

*Important statistics*
Temperature, humidity and ventilation are all closely related. Fortunately, provided manufacturer's instructions are followed, an acceptable level of hatching should result. Vital statistics for incubation and rearing are as follows:

### INCUBATION

| Week | Ducks temp | Geese temp | Ducks and Geese Humidity |
|------|-----------|-----------|--------------------------|
| 1 | 99.2$^0$ F (37.3$^0$ C) | 99.0$^0$ F (37.2$^0$ C) | Dry Bulb |
| 2 | 99.2$^0$ F (37.3$^0$ C) | 99.0$^0$ F (37.2$^0$ C) | 99.8$^0$ F (37.7$^0$ C) |
| 3 | 99.0$^0$ F (37.2$^0$ C) | 98.5$^0$ F (36.9$^0$ C) | Wet Bulb |
| 4 | — | 98.5$^0$ F (36.9$^0$ C) | 87.9$^0$ F (31$^0$ C) |

The temperature reading will depend on the type of machine. When a *separate* hatcher is used the eggs are transferred 3 days before hatching and the humidity is increased for the last 2 days. However, each machine is different so the precise instructions must depend on the maker's handbook.

## REARING

### Ducks and geese

| Week | ⁰ F | ⁰ C |
|------|-----|-----|
| 1 | 95 | 35 |
| 2 | 86 | 30 |
| 3 | 77 | 25 |

All writers on waterfowl hatching emphasize the need for a high level of humidity. However, if still-air machines are opened too frequently there is a danger of over-evaporation of eggs, even with a very high humidity.

In connection with rearing ducklings and goslings it should be noted that in the late spring and the summer the sooner they are taken off heat, the better they will be. Indeed, quite often a compartment lined with hay will give sufficient heat after the first week or two, so no artificial heat is necessary. Remember, though, that if there is any danger from frost some form of heat will be essential to keep the young stock warm during the night.

# CHAPTER 3

## SWANS

I shall not describe the young in down or the eggs of each species, my object being to furnish a ready guide to the identification of full-fledged birds such as the fancier will find offered for sale. Swans are easily recognised by their very long necks, bare faces, short legs, and large feet. They are all large, and essentially surface-feeders in habit, not diving, and walking awkwardly on land. They are omnivorous feeders, and are best turned out to fend for themselves on a large piece of water, where they will be of service in removing weeds; but they are also very destructive to fish spawn. When they need hand-feeding, the usual grain may be given; for the young, crushed Spratt's biscuits, stale bread, and groats may be thrown on the water. They should be allowed to manage their own nesting and rearing arrangements, being well able to look after their cygnets, and, indeed, dangerous to interfere with. More than one pair should not be kept on one piece of water, unless it is very large. The best-known species are the common white and the black swans.

## THE MUTE OR TAME SWAN

### (Cygnus olor)

This is the best known of all ornamental Waterfowl, and the earliest introduced, if it is true that it was first brought to England by our warrior monarch, Richard the Lion-hearted, who may thus claim to have been a fancier, like King Solomon, who imported Peacocks to adorn his court. And through all succeeding centuries the chaste and stately beauty of this noble bird has secured its position as the king of ornamental fowl. It is distinguished from all other Swans by the bare skin of the face and the knob of the bill being black, while the bill itself, except the

18

nostrils, edges, and top, which are also black, is orange red. The female is smaller, floats lower in the water, and has a slighter neck than her mate; she is known as the "pen", the male being the "cob". The cygnets are grey at first, with grey knobless bills, and do not become white till two years old. But there is a variety known as the Polish Swan, and formerly considered a distinct species, in which the cygnets are white from the first, while the knob of the bill is smaller and the feet paler than in the typical bird. This variety breeds true and should be encouraged, as the cygnets do not have to pass through any "ugly duckling" stage, but assume almost their full beauty with their first feathering. It should be noted that cygnets in their first year, if well fed, are very good eating.

The Mute Swan ranges across Europe to South-eastern Siberia and North-western India, where it is rare, Swans being imported from Europe and sold at high prices to wealthy natives. It is doubtfully wild in England, so many unpinioned birds being at large, but it breeds in a truly wild state no further off than Denmark and South Sweden. The young are generally hatched in England about the end of May, and during the breeding season the old birds are very vicious, and should be approached with caution. They attack with their wings, having little power in the bill.

## THE BLACK SWAN

### (Chenopis atrata)

This species, now one of the best known ornamental birds, is, as everybody knows, a native of Australia. It is considerably smaller and slighter than the common Swan, though it will boldly stand up to that bird on occasion. There is no knob on the bill, the neck is particularly long, and rather shaggily feathered, and the inner wing feathers are elegantly crimped. The plumage is coal black with white flights, and red bill, and bare streak on the face. I can find no description of the first plumage, but believe it is merely lighter.

The black swan ought to be kept more largely than it is. Being smaller and a better walker, it needs less water than the common swan, and from its colour does not soil in a smoky atmosphere,

19

*Figure 3-1*  Swans
    (a) Whooper
    (b) Bewicks
    (c) Mute

while it has a quaint grace of form peculiarly its own, and a pleasant note, quite unlike the snuffling croak of its otherwise more dignified rival.

It is also a very good breeder, will bring off two broods a year, and may breed in almost any month and rear young in mid-winter. It has never become very cheap, so would pay to rear better than the white.

The ordinary wild swans of England, the Whooper *(Cygnus musicus)* and Bewick's Swan *(Cygnus bewicki),* are not so often kept; both are white when adult, with knobless bills, black at the end and bright yellow at the root, this colour extending over the bare skin of the face. The young are grey. Their carriage is far less graceful than that of the Mute and Black Swans, as they keep their necks straight. Bewick's Swan is smaller and has less yellow on the bill than the Whooper.

Other less common swans are the beautiful Black-necked Swan *(Cygnus melancoryphus)* of South America, with its white body beautifully set-off by its black neck and grey bill, with a red knob and face-patch; it is about the size of the black swan.

Another South American swan, the Coscoroba *(Coscoroba candida)* is now often offered for sale; it is only as big as a small goose, white with black tips to the flights, and pinky-red bill and feet; there is no bare patch on the face in this species, and its neck is shorter and its legs longer than usual; but it has the true swan carriage.

# CHAPTER 4

## THE TRUE GEESE

Geese are very widely kept on ornamental waters, but they require a wide range to show to advantage and not interfere with each other. They are mostly land-birds in habit, not swimming so much as the rest of their family, and vegetarian feeders, living mainly on grass. Male and female are alike, and both tend the goslings, which, with the sitting, may well be left in their charge. If kept in enclosures, only one pair should be put in each, and plenty of grazing space allowed. It will be seen that on the whole they are only suitable where there is plenty of room. The old birds should receive some grain daily as well as their grazing, and the goslings bread-crumbs and meal. Geese all have short stout bills, with the nostrils in the centre, and stand high on the legs; they walk well, with a peculiar swaying gait, and swim very high in the stern. They are all brown or grey in plumage, with lighter edgings to the body-feathers, and white sterns. The young are much like the old birds. Most will breed well in captivity, and all nest on the ground. They are, of course, good eating, but the fancy breeds will hardly "go to pot!"

## THE GREY GOOSE

Under this head I propose to treat several species of British Geese, which are not among the most popular ornamental kinds, and which it would be a waste of space to describe separately. First, we have the Grey-lag, the ancestor of our tame European Geese *(Anser ferus)*. This bird is distinguished by its flesh-coloured feet and French-grey shoulders; the bill is either flesh-coloured or orange, without any black. It will cross readily with its descendant, the tame goose, than which it is considerably smaller in size, and, of course, lighter in make.

Then the Bean-goose *(Anser fabalis),* a dark-brown, slight-built

22

bird, smaller than the Grey-lag, with orange legs and bill, the latter black at the root and tip.

Smaller than this is the White-fronted Goose *(Anser albifrons)*, with orange feet and yellow or flesh-coloured bill; its general colour is brown, with a white patch on the forehead and black blotches on the belly.

About the same size is the Pink-footed Goose *(Anser brachy-rhynchus)*, coloured much like the Grey-lag, with a small bill, black at root and tip, and pink in the middle, the feet also being pink. This bird sometims occurs with orange on the bill and feet, but then its plumage and small bill will distinguish it from the dark, coarse-billed Bean-goose.

These geese have, of course, a wide range outside England, and only one, the Grey-lag, breeds in this country, and that only in Scotland. To its resident habits it owes its name, being the "lagging" goose which stayed to breed when the rest had left England for the North. It was tamed by the Greeks even in Homer's time, that poet mentioning "a large white goose, a tame bird from the yard". The white colour was thus early bred, and it is remarkable how little variation, comparatively speaking, has taken place in the tame goose under cultivation. It has, however, besides the more ordinary Embden and Toulouse breeds, familiar to most frequenters of poultry shows, produced one very curious variety.

## THE SEBASTOPOL GOOSE

This bird is rather smaller than ordinary tame geese, and white in colour, with blue eyes and orange or fleshy bill and feet. Its great peculiarity is in the lengthened, twisted, and frayed-out plumage of the body and inner part of the wings, which forms a regular fleece, even sometimes reaching the ground. The flights are defective, so that the birds cannot fly, as most geese, even though tame, can do. These birds are to my mind more curious than ornamental, but always attract notice, and perhaps deserve a place as freaks in any mixed collection. They should not, of course, be crossed.

Returning to more normal birds, we come to the second domestic species of goose, which has a rather uncertain status between ornamental waterfowl and poultry. This is:

# THE CHINESE GOOSE

## *(Cygnopsis cygnoides)*

The Chinese goose is always distinguishable from the common domestic goose by its longer neck, without the pleating of feathers of that part seen in the ordinary bird, and more upright carriage. It also has a knob on the bill, larger in the gander than in the goose. It is often white, with orange bill and feet, but when normally coloured is brown, not grey, with the top of the head and back of the neck uniform dark brown, the rest of the head and neck being pale buff. The bill in such birds is black, the feet only being orange. This is the coloration of the wild bird as it exists in Eastern Asia, but in this state it has a longer bill with no knob, and is, of course, much lighter in make, many tame Chinese geese being very broad in the stern, and paunchy and dewlapped like the Toulouse breed of the grey goose. Personally, I should prefer the lighter birds for ornamental purposes. Practically, the Chinese goose is of value as a very good layer, and an excellent alarm, though one may have too much of its vociferous screaming. It is fonder of the water than the common goose; when I had the opportunity of observing both species in a large park, I always noticed the Chinese kept nearer to the bank of the lake. They also take wing more readily, but are too tame to need pinioning or clipping. Exceptional scientific interest attaches to the Chinese goose in that, although so different in voice, habits, build and colour from our other domestic species, it has been known for the last century to produce fertile hybrids with it. The hybrid favours the Chinese in appearance.

The late Mr E. Blyth, one of the few naturalists who studied tame as well as wild birds, considered that the ordinary domestic goose of India was such a hybrid, and geese differing little from the wild Chinese, except in their rather coarser make, are often seen in the Calcutta market, where I have never seen one like an English bird, so that the Chinese blood must be very prepotent.

# THE BAR-HEADED GOOSE

## *(Anser indicus)*

This handsome goose comes as its specific name implies, from

Plate 1   SWANS AND GEESE

1. Mute Swan
2. Black Swan
3. Whooper Swan
4. Black-Necked Swan
5. Ross's Goose
6. Snow Goose

Plate 2  GEESE

1. Chinese Goose
2. Canada Goose
3. Red-Breasted Goose
4. Magellan Goose ♀ & ♂

5. Barnacle Goose
6. Egyptian Goose
7. Emperor Goose
8. Maned Goose
(or Australian Wood Duck)

Plate 3   SHELDUCKS

1. White-Faced Tree Duck
2. Fulvous Tree Duck
3. Paradise Duck

4. Australian Radjah Shelduck
5. Common Shelduck
6. Ruddy Shelduck

Plate 4  POCHARD AND PERCHING DUCKS

1. Canvas Back
2. Harlequin Duck
3. Carolina Duck

4. Mandarin Duck
5. Barrow's Goldeneye
6. Goldeneye

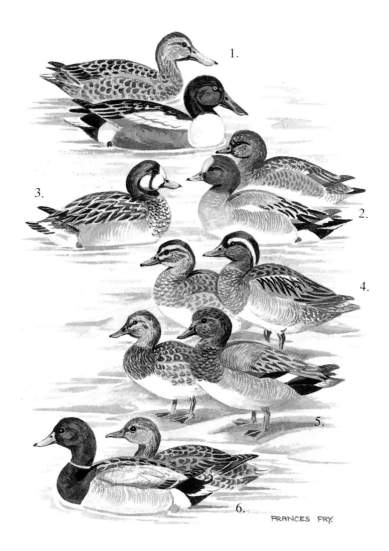

Plate 5   DABBLING DUCKS

1. Shoveler
2. Wigeon
3. Chiole Wigeon

4. Garganey
5. Gadwall
6. Mallard

Plate 6   PINTAIL, LONG-TAILED DUCK AND TEAL

1. Pintail
2. Long-Tailed Duck (or Old Squaw)
3. European Teal
4. Ringed Teal
5. Falceated Teal
6. Marbled Teal

Plate 7   SCOTERS, MERGANSERS AND STIFF-TAILS

1. Red-Breasted Merganser
2. Hooded Merganser
3. Surf Scoter

4. Goosander
5. Ruddy Duck
6. Smew

Plate 8  EIDERS AND POCHARD

1. Eider
2. King Eider
3. Ferruginous Duck (or White-eye)
4. Tufted Duck
5. Red-Crested Pochard
6. Rosybill

*Figure 4-1* Brent and Barnacle Geese

India, which country it inhabits only in the winter, going to Central Asia to breed. It has been imported rather freely of late, and is one of the most desirable of all geese as an ornamental bird, being of light, graceful build, with a small neat bill and clear French-grey plumage, a coloration rare among waterfowl. A dark brown stripe runs down the back of the neck, and is separated from the colour of the throat and breast by a white band; the head is white with two black bars across it at the back. The bill is yellow with a black tip, and the feet orange. Young birds do not show the head-marking.

## THE CANADA GOOSE

### (Branta canadensis)

This is one of our oldest-established ornamental waterfowl, being often allowed to go at large unpinioned, and is not unfrequently shot in a wild state in Europe, though originally a native of North America. It is a large goose, though not so big as the tame bird, and dark brown in body-colour, with a coal-black head and neck, set off by a white crescent across the throat; the bill and feet are black. In young birds the white feathers of the throat are edged with black.

When this goose has a good range it may be allowed to go at large unpinioned; I remember, when a boy, often seeing a flock in this condition, and very ornamental they were. But, of course, the fancier who allows his geese the use of their wings must be prepared to risk their straying and getting shot, though their ornamental appearance is a great inducement to hazard this. This goose will breed with the two species of tame geese.

## THE BARNACLE GOOSE

### (Branta leucopsis)

This is a rather small goose, with a peculiarly small and delicate bill. Its colour is very striking, the face being white, the neck black, and the body clear grey, the feathers having a black bar before the usual pale tip, this double marking producing a very elegant appearance. The bill and feet are black. The young show some black on the white face.

The Barnacle visits England and other European countries in winter, but its breeding haunts have not yet been made out. In captivity it breeds well, and the young may be allowed their liberty unpinioned. It has bred with the Canada Goose in a free state, and with the White-fronted Goose in captivity.

## THE BRENT GOOSE

### *(Branta bernicla)*

This pretty little bird is much smaller than the other geese I have mentioned, being no bigger than a common duck. It is dark grey in colour, with a black head and neck, the latter being set off by a patch of white mingled with black, on each side near the head; the breast is black, and the stern white, as is usual in geese. Young birds are paler, and have no white on the neck.

This bird breeds in the Arctic regions all round the world, migrating south in winter, at which season it is the commonest British Wild Goose; it is almost entirely a sea-coast bird, feeding on sea-grass and other marine vegetation. It is possible for this reason, that it has not been bred in confinement, for it is frequently kept and lives very well. It is recommended by its neat though sombre appearance, and conveniently small size, to those who have not room for the bigger geese.

It will be obvious from what has been said above that there is a wide field open for the goose fancier. Geese need little water, breed well as a rule, have constantly pleasing if quiet plumage, and, from their greater steadiness, are more suitable for exhibition than ducks. Given a good grass run, no birds will give less trouble or repay it better.

## CHAPTER 5

## CEREOPSIS, MAGELLAN, AND EGYPTIAN GEESE

The three birds to be dealt with in the present chapter are very different from the true geese, although they go popularly under the same name; indeed, the last two are, strictly speaking, not geese at all, but simply overgrown ducks, agreeing with these birds in their brilliant colours and in the difference of voice in the sexes; in connection with which it is to be noted that the males of these species, like drakes, have a bony bulb attached to the base of the windpipe, the result of this arrangement being to considerably modify the voice. All require the same general treatment as geese, but unless they can be given an absolutely free range had better be kept apart, owing to infirmities of temper, for which they are notorious.

## THE CEREOPSIS GOOSE

### *(Cereopsis novæ hollandiæ)*

If this remarkable bird really is a goose, it certainly does not very closely resemble its relatives. In form it is short-necked, stout-billed, and high on the legs, these members being strong, with the feet only partially webbed, and furnished with large strong claws. The wings are comparatively short, not long as in the true geese. In fact, among these geese this bird recalls the Indian Game and Aseel amongst fowls by its light yet powerful build. The bill is short and thick, the end being horny and black, and the rest covered with a waxy skin or "cere" as in birds of prey, these being of a greenish-yellow colour. The plumage is grey, with black tips to the flights and black tail, and a creamy patch on the top of the head. The eyes are bright red and the legs brick red, the feet and claws being black. Both sexes are similar, the female, as in true geese, being smaller, and the young exhibiting the

*Figure 5-1* Magellan Geese

characteristic cere at birth, and closely resembling old birds when feathered.

The Cereopsis is a native of Australia, but has long been introduced into Europe, and is not frequently shown. They are said to have a vile temper, and to attack not only other waterfowl, but domestic animals of small size and even human beings, so that they should be lodged away from other pets and out of the way of children. Were it not for this unfortunate failing, *Cereopsis* would suit very many people, needing less water than any others of their kind, for they are very much more land birds than waterfowl, running well and swimming awkwardly; in fact, judging from what I saw of them for some time at the London Zoo, I should say that practically they only take to water to wash, and that therefore a large tub would be all the accommodation they require. They breed from March to May, lay about five eggs, and sit thirty-five days.

## THE MAGELLAN OR UPLAND GOOSE

### *(Chloephaga magellanica)*

This beautiful bird is as distinct from the true geese in form as it is in the marked difference between the sexes. It stands very high on the leg, the thighs, which are well feathered, being prominent; the shanks are also unusually long, and the feet small and not quite fully webbed; the bill is very small but goose-like in form, with central nostrils. The gander is mostly white with a grey back, black and white tail, and black barring on the flanks. The goose, which is smaller and not so reachy in build, is brown where the gander is white, and barred all over below. She also has bright yellow legs, while the gander's are black, as is the bill in both sexes. Both birds also agree in the wings, which have white "shoulders", black flights, and metallic green secondary quills, forming a bright bar when the wing is closed. In first feather the young more resemble the goose, but the yellow legs of the females show early. This very showy bird inhabits the southern part of South America, but was introduced into Europe more than fifty years ago, and breeds well, nesting in the spring on the ground under a low bush, and laying four to eight eggs, which are incubated for about a month. It is said to be a great coward in the company of other geese, and is certainly a bully with smaller waterfowl, so should be well looked after if placed in a mixed collection. Although not positively awkward in the water, it does not look its best there, and is far more attractive on land, where its motions are easy and graceful. A small pond for washing purposes is all it really needs, and, given this, it would be difficult to find handsomer ornaments for a paddock than a pair of these fine birds, both sexes of which are equally beautiful in their own way. The goose has a much stronger voice than the gander, but they are not unpleasantly noisy like many of the true geese.

A very similar but rarer species is the Chilian Upland Goose *(Chloephaga inornata),* in which the male is much more barred than the common kinds, while the female has a dull grey instead of brown head. The similarity of the amount of pencilling in the two sexes naturally renders this species more pleasing to the eye of a fancier who likes uniformity.

## THE EGYPTIAN GOOSE

### *(Chenalopex ægyptiacus)*

This well-known species is simply an overgrown member of the group of species of Sheldrakes, next to be mentioned; it is slighter in build than the true geese, and more leggy, while the bill is somewhat intermediate in form between a goose's and a duck's. It is a good big bird, more than two feet long from bill to tail. In colour it is brown above and pencilled buff below and on the flanks; the head and neck are whitey-brown with a chestnut patch round each eye; there is a large chestnut patch also on the breast; the flights and tail are black, the shoulder of the wing white with a narrow black stripe a little way in front of the dark metallic green wingbar. The eyes are yellow, and the bill and feet pink. The female is like the male, but smaller and not quite so bright, and the young are very similar.

This African bird is of very old introduction as an ornamental waterfowl, and has often been shot at large in England, even so long ago as 1823, when five were killed. In spite of the warm climate it naturally inhabits, it is quite hardy and a very free breeder, and the young, if there is a wide range, may be suffered to go at large unpinioned, subject to the risk of getting shot if they wander away. It is a good easy bird to begin upon, but not a good companion for other species, as it has a peculiarly nasty temper, and will tackle a human being, if seized, with a vigour sufficient to draw blood, besides striking savagely with the wings. It should therefore be given a place to itself, if almost unlimited space is not available. In a wild state it nests on cliffs and trees, and the young are said to be fond of locusts. The voice of the male is a low husky chatter; of the female, a harsh, unpleasant barking quack.

Altogether the Egyptian goose is a bird rather of the "cheap and nasty" order, chiefly suitable to people who want to ornament large grounds with small trouble and expense. For such a purpose, the showy colours and readiness to breed which characterise this bird render it very suitable. It lays at the beginning of spring, and sits four weeks on four to eight eggs. Since it is so easily bred, some selection might well be attempted in order to produce a race less pugnacious than the present one, for it is notorious that domesticated birds, unless bred for fighting, are not so pugilistic as those which have only comparatively recently been reclaimed.

# CHAPTER 6

## SHELDUCKS

These fine birds which are universally regarded as ducks, are of considerably more interest to the ordinary fancier than their bigger relatives. The Shelducks are ducks of large size, being as big as or bigger than the ordinary wild duck. They are much more elegant in make than ducks generally, having small neat bills, long wings, rather long square tails, and comparatively light bodies, standing high on rather long legs. They move about much on land, where they are more active and graceful than any other ducks, but they also swim well, sitting high on the water with the stern well up, like the geese. In disposition they are intelligent and courageous — rather too much so, in fact, for in the breeding season they may be a source of danger even to larger birds. Their colours are very handsome, and have the great advantage of being nearly equally brilliant in both sexes; and there is no summer change in the drakes. Three species are easily obtainable, and they are highly to be recommended to anyone who wants a pair of handsome birds for his garden, for they only need a small pond, and their size secures them against ordinary small vermin. Moreover, they will all breed in captivity. They are omnivorous feeders, but need much green food.

## THE COMMON SHELDUCK

### *(Tadorna cornuta)*

This is the smallest of the three, and the most gaily coloured of all the ducks, being conspicuous at a great distance, especially as it sits very high in the water, almost like a gull. The general plumage is pure white, the head being deep green, and the flights, tip of tail, a long patch on each side of the back, and another down the belly, black. A broad chestnut belt crosses the breast and shoulders, and the stern and innermost quills are also chestnut; the wing-bar is bright green. The bill is beautiful bright red, and the legs flesh-coloured. The drake is larger and brighter, and during the breeding season has a knob at the root of the bill, but otherwise is like the duck; and the young birds in first plumage cannot be mistaken for any other species, though wanting the green gloss on the head and the chestnut and black on the lower parts. The bill also is merely of a livid flesh-colour in the young, not becoming red till later.

This is the best tempered of all the Shelducks, though it should not be trusted in too close quarters with other waterfowl, being able to make itself unpleasant even to a goose, as I have seen in St. James's Park, where it has bred. This Shelduck inhabits the northern part of the old world in summer, migrating south in winter, and generally frequenting the sea coast. It is one of the few ducks that breed in England. The nest is placed in a hole, and this habit must be considered if one wishes to breed the bird in captivity, in which state the Shelduck does well — a remarkable fact when it is considered that it is mainly a salt water bird and naturally feeds on shell-fish and seaweed, instead of grain and grass. As above stated, common Sheldrakes will breed well enough if given a burrow to nest in, and are not so spiteful as some of their kin, while the brilliant contrasts of their even-marked plumage are sure to excite admiration. Moreover, the birds become very tame. I have even had one eat out of my hand at the Clifton Zoo, where they have, or had some years ago, a nice lot of waterfowl loose in a big pond with cruelly steep cemented sides, which was hard on the poor birds, fed, as they were, out of the water. Altogether this Shelduck stands as much apart among ducks for beauty, style, and character, as the Goldfinch does among Finches, and I wonder that it is not more kept.

## THE RUDDY SHELDUCK

### *(Casarca rutila)*

This is a bigger bird than the preceding, with a straighter bill, the common Shelduck's bill being concave or "dished" in profile. Its colour, though less striking than that of its ally, is very fine, being a rich golden cinnamon, darkening to chestnut on the belly and paling to buff on the head and neck; this is set off by a black rump, flights, and tail, while the wing bar is bronze green and the "shoulder" and lining of the wing white. The bill, feet and eyes are black. The duck differs from the drake in having a white face, and in never assuming a black ring round the base of the buff neck which he wears in summer; she is, of course, smaller.

The young are much like old birds, but duller, and it should be mentioned that among birds of the same age, apparently there is in this species a remarkable variation in colour from the rich hue above described to a washy mottled buff most unpleasing to the eye. Possibly, as in domestic birds of similar hue, some are naturally bad and unsound in colour. On the other hand, the white shoulders may be tinged with buff, which is, in my opinion, a fault, as the contrast of the pure white with the red and black, seen when the bird flaps its wings, and only then, is so beautiful.

The Ruddy Shelduck is also an old-world bird, but has a more southern range than the common Shelduck. It is very common in India in winter, and many are exported thence to Europe. Its common name in India is the "Brahminy Duck", and it has a bad reputation among duck shooters for spoiling sport by its wariness which alarms other fowls. Among the natives, however, it has a semi-sacred character. A legend, indeed, tells that the Brahminy ducks, which are usually seen in pairs, are the present habitations of the souls of a sort of Hindu Romeo and Juliet, doomed for their rebellious love always to remain apart on opposite sides of a river, while their call is rendered as a constant appeal from one to be allowed to join the other, an application which is always refused. And, indeed, as a well-known Indian naturalist, Mr E. C. S. Baker, has pointed out, it needs little imagination to hear in the broken trumpet call of this Sheldrake the Hindustani equivalent for the lover's appeal — *Ahna sukta, Chukwa? Nai, Chuckwi* (May I come, Chukwa? No, Chukwi), etc. And as *Chukwa-chukwi* the bird is commonly known. But to descend from romance to practice; happy or unhappy themselves, Chukwa and Chukwi have tempers of their own, and will make matters lively enough for any other waterfowl, smaller or larger, that may be unfortunate enough to be confined closely with them, even if not breeding. On the other hand, they breed well themselves, spend most of their time on land, and their colour looks peculiarly beautiful on grass — on which they graze readily, so that they are particularly suited to a beginner who wants to take no trouble, especially as they are not expensive. If the young be allowed to grow up unpinioned, they will probably be lost in time; but the experiment is worth making, as no duck is so beautiful on the wing, the contrast of the cinnamon body and pied wings, well seen in the show flight, being remarkably striking. I well remember the fine sight which four unpinioned birds of this species, bred in St. James's Park some years ago, used to present when on the wing, seen against a background of dark green foliage. As the Ruddy Sheldrake breeds in any sort of hole in rocks, or even deserted buildings, it ought to be possible, if people can ever be got to leave out of the way birds alone, to have it flying about houses like a pigeon, as it has not the love of salt water to tempt it away — this probably being the reason why the common Sheldrake cannot be got to stay. This bird is an early breeder, producing a nest of eggs even in snowy March. The eggs are cream coloured, from seven to twelve in number.

This bird has hybridized with the Egyptian goose, which, as above stated, is really only a big Sheldrake. A pair of these mules used to be on view at the London Zoo. They almost completely resemble the Ruddy Sheldrake, though larger and duller, but had the pink legs of the other parent. I have seldom seen such one-sided hybrids.


## THE VARIEGATED SHELDUCK OR PARADISE DUCK

### (Casarca variegata)

This species resembles the last in size, style, and colour of bill, feet and wings, but differs much in the body plumage of the male, which is of a dark pencilled iron-grey, set off by a chestnut stern and inner quills, and a dark glossy green head. The female is much more like the Ruddy Shelduck, but has pencilled grey mixed with the red, and a pure white head: the sexes, though equally handsome, being very unlike each other, a unique case among the Sheldrakes. The young birds of both sexes are alike, and more closely resemble the drake, the young ducks getting their white heads at about six months old.

This native of New Zealand is not, to my mind, nearly such a handsome bird as either of its relatives, and is rather flattered by its second name. However, it is showy enough, and the usual contrast between the sexes will be a recommendation to some people. Fanciers have found this bird peculiarly bad tempered during the breeding season, a pair belonging to a lady having deliberately attempted to murder a Canadian gander, and nearly succeeded! A more creditable instance of the bond between the pair is mentioned by Sir W. Buller in his *Birds of New Zealand,* where he mentions having seen a drake gallantly beat off a large Hawk from his wounded mate.

The same author states that this duck is liable to violent and ultimately fatal attacks of cramp if denied access to water, although, like others of its kind, it is quite at home on land, and walks and runs well. It is considerably more expensive than the other species, and so it should pay them to breed, which they appear to do in our spring, in spite of their Antipodean home, but this no doubt applies to European bred birds only. Speaking of the breeding of Shelducks, a curious case occurred in the London Zoo many years ago. An unmated female of the rare African Ruddy Sheldrake, *(Casarca cana),* which closely resembles the Eastern bird above described, paired with a male Common Shelduck, and the hybrids were dark pencilled grey birds, much like the New Zealand drake. Now, considering that all the Shelducks are obviously nearly related, it seems possible that this was a case of "throwing back", and that the present duck, with its similar ally, the Australian Shelduck *(Casarca tadornoides),* a bird very rarely imported, represents the ancestor of the whole Sheldrake genus.

# CHAPTER 7

## MUSCOVY, MANDARIN, AND CAROLINA DUCKS

The three varieties to be dealt with in this section all agree in being ducks of surface-feeding habit and of strong perching proclivities, also nesting in trees in the natural state. In form they are rather noteworthy for their rather short bills, crested heads, short legs, and long, broad tails, the last being very characteristic. All are very well known and always to be had, breeding well in confinement.

## THE MUSCOVY DUCK

### *(Cairina moschata)*

This bird, like the Chinese goose, occupies a debatable ground between poultry and ornamental waterfowl. A native of tropical America, it is found all over the world in a tame state, and was tame when the Spaniards invaded its native country, though the wild stock still exists there. This is black in colour, with a rich beetle green and purple gloss above, and the "shoulders" and lining of the wings white. There is a red wattle round the eye (extending to the base of the beak) in the drake, but this is wanting in the duck, which is very much smaller. Both sexes have the same plumage, and possess a crest, which, however, is not visible unless erected, as it frequently is when the bird is excited.

Many tame birds have the coloration above described, though usually showing some white feathers about the head and neck; some are all black and some pied, a white variety with a black crest being known as the "Peruvian". Pure white is also found, and a blue-grey like that of an Andalusian fowl, though this last is rare. The tame duck of this species shows the face-wattle like the drake, though it is not so well developed; similarly the tame hen has a good-sized comb, though this is almost wanting in the female of the original Jungle-fowl.

In England the Muscovy is treated usually as an ornamental bird, and, though I am rather peculiar, I fear, in my liking for it, I think much may be said in its favour. For ornament I like the typical colour best, as I think one cannot improve on nature; and the white birds, with their blue eyes and sickly-yellow bills and feet, are to my mind much more curious than pretty. I like a moderate amount only of eye-wattle, and this is all the better if broken and varied with black. But whatever colour is fancied for ornamental Muscovies, a coarse paunchy bird should be avoided, for the deep keel so much favoured by breeders of the larger varieties of the common duck looks utterly out of place with the long low form of this species.

The great advantage of the Muscovy is that it can be allowed full liberty, although it retains the power of flight, and is, indeed, still rather fond of perching; but it is sluggish and not apt to stray. It is also a very silent bird; the duck seldom quacks, and then not loudly, while the drake only puffs and hisses in a ludicrous manner. Against these good qualities must be set the fact that the drake of this species is very quarrelsome and unduly amative, his great size and strength rendering him a great nuisance on this account. For this reason, Muscovies should only be kept with the larger ducks, geese, etc., and not with the weaker species; several ducks should also be allowed to one drake.

But it seems to me that the merits of the Muscovy as a useful bird are not sufficiently appreciated in England. True, although young birds are good, an old drake is most tough and objectionable food; moreover, although he attains a great weight, even up to fifteen pounds, his partner is only about two-thirds his size. But the true value of this species lies in its readiness to hybridise with the common ducks, for the hybrids thus obtained are of large size and excellent flavour, and do not differ in bulk according to sex more than ordinary ducks as a rule. Although favouring the common duck in colour and absence of face wattle, they have the Muscovy carriage, power of flight, and perching habits. They are, as might be expected, barren, but this is no disadvantage when they are to be used as food; and it seems to me that making this cross would be the best way of fairly utilising the Indian Runner breed of the common duck, whose active foraging habits and laying powers are at present somewhat discounted by its small size, a fault easily removed by this method. It seems that mule ducks of this sort are commonly raised in France. I have possessed several in India, and both observed and eaten them. Of course, for raising table hybrids the white Muscovy would be best. The Muscovy duck is a fair layer, the eggs being white, and a better mother than the common duck; she often nests high up, according to her natural habit. Muscovies care less for water than common ducks — another practical advantage. Their name, by the way, is said to have no reference to the old word for Russia, but is thought to be a corruption of Musky duck, the oil gland on the drake's tail distinctly exhaling a musky odour.

With the Muscovy duck ends the series of large vicious birds which need space and often separate accommodation; all the species which follow are quiet with others on the whole, and may be kept together in one enclosure, though, as a rule it is best not to have more than one pair of each kind. Most of these I shall treat of now are considerably smaller than the common wild duck, and they include the species commonly shown.

## THE MANDARIN DUCK

### (Aix galericulata)

This species is the most popular of all the small ornamental waterfowl, and no wonder, for, excluding the Pheasant family, no bird known to the fancier is so showy as the drake of this species, nor is any more eccentrically decorated among them all. In size the Mandarin is small, only about seventeen inches long; in build he is very like a miniature Muscovy, but stands higher on the legs, and is more abundantly "furnished" than any known duck, having a long crest, a ruff of hackles round the neck, and the inner web of the innermost quill of each wing developed into a fan shape, and about three inches broad — an ornament which will distinguish him from any bird whatever. He is just as eccentric in colour as in form; the crest is copper and green, the face is buff, shading to white as it passes back to the crest, the hackles bright cinnamon, the wing fan also cinnamon, bordered with white and

*Figure 7-1*  Mandarin Drake and Duck

black behind and steel-blue below; the flanks are pencilled-buff and the breast maroon, divided in the middle by the white of the belly and stern, and separated from the flanks by two bars each of white and black. The back and tail are green glossed brown, with a long splash of steel-blue down each side of the former; and the wings, except for the fan, are of a similar metallic brown with a purple bar and silver-grey edgings to the flights, which are tipped with steel-blue on the inner web. The eyes, which are unusually large for a duck, are dark, the small bill rose-pink, and the feet yellow with black webs.

The duck has no wing-fans nor hackle, and but a small crest, but her neat head, large dark eyes, and graceful shape make her a noticeably pretty bird, although she does not show the pencilling so common in the females of the duck tribe, being plain brown above, mottled with buff on the breast, and white below, with a white ring round the eye. The outsides of the flights are silvered as in the drake, and the insides dark — a marking which easily distinguishes her from any other duck except the Carolina, of which more hereafter. Her bill is dull horn colour, and the feet duller than the drake's.

The drake undergoes a very complete summer change in this species, becoming almost exactly like his mate, and losing all his furnishing. He often, however, retains his pink bill. When he does not, the duck may be distinguished by having the blue wing-bar bordered *below* as well as behind with white. With this exception, the young drake is like the young duck.

The Mandarin is a native of Eastern Asia — central and southern China, Formosa, and Japan: Amoorland, in Siberia, it visits only in the breeding season. Although thus affecting warm or temperate countries, it is a hardy bird, and few ducks are more ready to breed in captivity, while it bears close confinement well. Indeed, a pair will live and breed in an enclosure six feet square — not that I should care to keep such birds in such close quarters, which are only fit in my opinion for a pair of Teal, or better, Moorhens or Dabchicks, if one *must* have waterfowl in such a small space. However, this contented disposition is much to the Mandarin's credit, and another good point about it is its great activity and energetic disposition. Whether on foot, walking or swimming, or on the wing, it is active in its movements, and it perches as readily as a pigeon. So marked is this propensity, that if these birds have to be confined at all it is far better to wire over the space and leave them unpinioned, as they will make excellent use of scope for flying. In this case, some dead branches should, of course, be set up for them to perch on, and the nesting-boxes should also be placed high up. Another attractive point about this lovely duck is that he is, more than any other species, "a bird of position", and much given to showing himself off, by raising his crest and slightly expanding his wings vertically, so as to bring the wing-fans perpendicular and display the beautifully striped flights, while, when standing, he often curves his neck back and throws out his breast like a Fantail pigeon. He certainly looks at such a time as if he were quite conscious of his beauty, and his little brown mate, as she caresses his orange hackles, must surely admire it. The affection between a pair of these birds is most marked; as above implied, they fondle each other's heads like pigeons, and they always keep together. The Mandarin is, however, a bird of character, and has strong likes and dislikes. Where several are kept together I have seen and heard that a favoured drake will attract more than one duck, while another will be left out in the cold, and in one case I myself witnessed their preference evidently went by the looks of the favourite.

The Mandarin drake must also be brave as well as beautiful, for he is a hard fighter with his own sex, and has even been known to kill a strange female put with him for exhibition purposes. It is well, therefore, not to put two breeding pairs of Mandarins in the same enclosure; with other ducks, even their near relative, the Carolina, they are quiet enough, though well able to look after themselves and hold their own with larger species. In fact, whether one considers its activity, courage, affection, and constitutional vigour, or its remarkably developed plumage, which strikes most people as an eccentric product of the Fancy rather than of nature, one must pronounce the Mandarin to be the ultimate development of the duck tribe.

The eggs of the Mandarin take 28-30 days to hatch, and as many as thirty may be laid in a season, if the first batch be taken away, though whether this forcing be desirable is another matter. The species is a favourite one for exhibition, and evidently needs show competition to keep it up to the mark in an artificial state. In the show pen it often has to compete with its only near ally and rival:

# THE CAROLINA DUCK

## (Aix sponsa)

This lovely bird, which some people prefer to the Mandarin, is of about the same size as that species, but lower on its legs, and of more level carriage, this approximating still more to the Muscovy, which it also somewhat recalls in gait and gesture, being less animated and less given to posturing than the Mandarin. Indeed, the drake has only one piece of furnishing to show off, his magnificent crest, which is deep, glossy purple and green, with two parallel longitudinal white streaks, one running from the bill and one from the eye. The rest of the head and neck are of the same rich metallic hue as the sides, the front being pure white, running up into a point on the cheeks and again below. All the upper plumage is resplendent with a satiny or velvety gloss of steel-blue and bronze-green, while the breast is rich chocolate with triangular white spots passing into the white of the belly, which, however, stops at the stern, this being dark and richly glossed like the upper parts. The flanks are pencilled as in the Mandarin, but on a cream instead of a buff ground and finished off with an edging of black and white, obliquely transverse bars above, which are barely indicated in the other species. Between flanks and tail comes a patch of rich maroon, and the flights are silvered and steel-tipped as in the Mandarin, while the similar blue, white-tipped wing-bar is almost lost in the general brilliancy of the wing. The bill is scarlet, yellow and black, the eyes and eyelids red, and the feet yellow, with dark webs.

The duck much resembles the Mandarin duck in colour, but shows above enough of the bronze and steel gloss of her mate to distinguish her on close inspection; moreover, the white round the eye spreads with age to the forehead and chin, and is always extensive. But the best point by which to distinguish the two ducks, if they can be taken in hand, is the wing-lining, which is coarsely pencilled in black and white in the Carolina, and plain grey-brown in the Mandarin.

It will be seen that the Carolina duck is a considerably better match for her mate than the Mandarin; and the drake himself makes some amends for his want of fans and hackle by not going into such complete undress as his relative. He loses his crest it is

44

true, but he still has a blackish-green head with white throat, and a fair amount of gloss on the upper surface, although no longer to be compared with what he was when in colour.

Thus each of these charming ducks has points of its own to recommend it to the fancier, one excelling in brilliant and bizarre ornamentation, the other having a more sober and richer beauty, and not exhibiting such a sombre appearance in the female and out-of-plumage male.

The Carolina duck, often called the Summer duck, is chiefly found in North America, but ranges south to the West Indies; in the States it is known as the Wood duck.

It has long been known as an ornamental bird, having been introduced early in the century. Its general habits and disposition resemble those of the Mandarin, and it should be treated in the same way; but in the show pen a Mandarin drake ought to take precedence of a Carolina of equal merit, seeing that his points are more numerous; while, on the other hand, the Carolina duck, if well glossed and with good face-marking, should have her claims considered as against her plainer rival if pairs are being shown. In fact, as the duck of this species shows a tendency to high colour, this should be encouraged by competition as much as possible by the showing of single birds.

# CHAPTER 8

## WHISTLERS (TREE DUCKS)

The group of Whistling or Tree ducks is one very distinct from all others, and when one member of it has been seen any can be easily recognised. The head and bill are ordinary enough, though the dark eyes are rather larger than usual, but the general build is very unlike that of other ducks, being light and reachy, with long neck and shanks, large feet, and long, prominent thighs set well back and close together. The tail is very short, and the wings, though broad and large for the size of the bird, are very short in the flights, which do not appear when the wing is closed. By this, and by the fact that the wings are black beneath, a Whistler may be known at once. The webs of the feet are not so full as in most ducks, and the hind toe is larger than is usually the case; altogether, these birds are rather intermediate in form between ducks and some of the waders. Their colours are very pretty and showy, though no brilliant or metallic hues occur; duck and drake are quite alike, and the young differ little if at all from them; there is no summer change. The Whistlers are found in warm climates only, but extend all round the world; they are ducks of singularly all-round abilities. Walking without the usual waddle, though with a very erect carriage on land, they are nevertheless good swimmers, and dive nearly as well as Pochards, like which birds (whose turn will come last of all) they often feed at the bottom, though in order to dive they make a spring which lifts their bodies clear of the surface, instead of going under easily and without effort. They fly slowly, as might be expected from their broad, hollow rounded wings; but this conformation gives them much more control over their flight in a small space; and they perch so readily that they are often known as tree ducks, nesting also in trees as a rule. Their call is a cackling whistle, similar in both sexes, whence their more appropriate name, since other ducks frequent trees, notably those of the section last dealt with.

They are not large birds, averaging about eighteen inches long.

Although no single species of this group equals several others in attractiveness, yet, taken as a group, no other ducks, in my opinion, come up to them. They are very easily tamed and kept, and interesting to watch, being very courageous and affectionate, like the Mandarin and Carolina, nor are they exacting as to accommodation. But they have two rather serious drawbacks. One is that they are not so hardy as other ducks, being, as above stated, denizens of warm climates only; the other is that, though so easily tamed, they are very hard to breed, only one species, and that the least attractive, having as yet nested in captivity*. This, however, ought only to stimulate fanciers to persevere with them; and as to their want of hardihood, this merely means they must be cared for under cover in winter like valuable poultry or pigeons, being given quarters in a warm, covered, sheltered run, well littered and furnished with perches — for owing to the necessity for taking them in in winter, it is quite unnecessary to pinion them, in my opinion. If this be done, however, the joint should not be cut as advised in my introductory section, as birds so treated may still be able to fly. Instead, the bone itself should be severed as close up to the pinion-joint as possible with a strong pair of scissors, this being, indeed, the method recommended by some authorities for all waterfowl, though, personally, I think this takes too much off in the case of long-flighted birds. And Whistlers, I think, should certainly be kept under netting unless they can have a big pond to range over, as they are better suited to aviary life than other ducks except Mandarins.

After this somewhat lengthy preliminary, I will proceed to the description of the various species at present available, which are four in number, and, resembling each other almost as closely as varieties of a breed of poultry or pigeons, will not detain us very long, thus making amends for previous prolixity.

## THE WHITE-FACED WHISTLER

### (Dendrocygna viduata)

This species, the prettiest of the lot, to my thinking, inhabits

*This may no longer apply, but ideal conditions are necessary for captive breeding to occur.

Tropical Africa and America, and is very showily marked; the face and throat are white, the rest of the head and neck black, the breast bright cinnamon, the flanks barred buff and black, divided by the black of the belly and stern; the rump, flights, and tail are also black, the rest of the wings slate with a reddish-cinnamon shoulder-patch, and the back dark brown laced with buff; the bill and feet are grey, as is generally the case with Whistlers.

This species is frequently shown, and, in addition to its striking plumage, has the recommendation of being more graceful in form and musical in voice than any of the other Whistlers: but I have heard that it is sometimes very pugnacious.

## THE RED-BILLED WHISTLER

### *(Dendrocygna autumnalis)*

This is also a very pretty bird, but not so graceful as the preceding; it has the webs of the feet less well developed than the rest. It inhabits the warm parts of America, and is often shown, being freely imported to Europe. The red bill and flesh-coloured feet will at once distinguish it from any other Whistler. The plumage is also characteristic, the general colour above being cinnamon-brown without bars or lacing, passing into pale drab on the sides of the head and neck. The underparts below the breast, the rump, flanks, flights, tail, and a streak down the back of the neck, are all black, with the exception of a white patch at the root of the flights, and of the stern, which is white spotted with black. Young birds are greyer above, and have the belly and flanks dirty white with dark bars.

## THE SMALL INDIAN WHISTLER

### *(Dendrocygna javanica)*

This is the smallest of the Whistlers and the plainest in colour, but is still a very neat and pretty little bird, abundant in the warm parts of Eastern Asia, where it ranges from India to Java. Its general colour is dun, shading into cinnamon on the belly. The back is slate barred with dun. The flights are black, and there is a reddish-cinnamon patch on the shoulder of the wing and at the

*Figure 8-1*   Red-billed Whistling Duck

root of the tail. The beak and feet are dark grey and the eyelids bright yellow, as in the Blackbird, beautifully setting off the dark eye. Young birds merely differ in having the underparts dun throughout. This duck is freely imported and very cheap, but unusually sensitive to cold.

## THE LARGE INDIAN WHISTLER

### *(Dendrocygna fulva)*

This species, also known as the Fulvous Duck, has a most peculiar range, being found in warm countries all round the world, in Africa, India and America, and is the only non-migratory bird which can say as much for itself except our own Barn Owl, which does not keep to warm countries only.

The Large Whistler has not much else to pride itself on, for it is a very ungainly-looking bird, the biggest of all the Whistlers, with a large coarse head, and positively enormous feet, like mud-boards. However, its coloration makes some amends, it being of a rich cinnamon, the beak black with cinnamon bars, and the wings mostly black. There is a black streak down the back of the neck, a cream bar at the root of the tail, and some cream splashes on the flanks. The feet are French grey, beautifully setting off the body-colour, and the bill a darker shade of grey.

On the whole, therefore, this Whistler-in-chief is not without its merits. Although the biggest of its race, it is not pugnacious, giving way to its smaller Indian relative, which is no doubt the reason why it is scarce in India.

Fanciers should aspire to breed Whistlers, remembering that these birds naturally nest aloft, the small Indian Whistler often using old nests of other birds, and carrying the ducklings down in her feet when the family has to be set afloat.

# CHAPTER 9

## THE MALLARD AND ITS ALLIES

In this chapter I propose to deal with our native wild duck and some of its tame descendants, together with the one wild species which is at once very nearly related and often kept, though it must be remembered that all the following species, until we come to the Pochards at the close, are near connections of the Mallard. All are surface feeders and ground builders, walking fairly well ashore, but with a waddling gait. In nearly all the drakes are finely pencilled and the ducks laced, and in most the drake undergoes the usual vexatious change of colour in summer; the young birds resemble the duck in their first feather.

## THE MALLARD

### *(Anas boscas)*

I ought to endeavour to save myself trouble by saying that this bird is too well known to need description; but as the species is apt to degenerate when bred in domestication, and may often be mongrelised when wild, like the Blue Rock pigeon, it is as well to characterise the points of the true Mallard. Although a big duck, nearly two feet long, and weighing up to three pounds, and rather heavy in make compared to many other species, the true wild bird has a very game, thoroughbred look compared with the tame one, being very tight in plumage, with a lean, game head, and comparatively small feet, a light body free from paunchiness, and long wings reaching nearly to the end of the tail. The general colour should be pencilled drab-grey, produced by fine brown lines on white; the head brilliant metallic green, the breast chocolate, and the rump, four curly centre tail feathers, and stern velvety green-black; the wings, plain drab with a steel-blue bar edged with white fore and aft. A white collar, which should be narrow, separates the green neck from the breast, not meeting

51

behind; and the pale drab tail shades into white at the edges. The lining of the wing is also white, and, with these exceptions, no plain white should be seen, nor any rusty tinge. The bill is yellowish green, and the feet orange with darker webs.

The duck to match should be dun laced with dark brown, with feet and wings like the drake's, and black bill with a broad orange tip. In undress the drake will be like her, but darker generally, and black on crown and rump. I think young drakes fledge off into this plumage, not exactly like the duck's, and I am inclined to believe that this is the case with other young drakes of this section also. But this is a point on which naturalists give us little information, and this must therefore, as in so many cases, be left for fanciers to supply.

The Mallard is one of several ducks which can give the northern hemisphere generally as their address, and judiciously resides in temperate climates, and visits the hot and cold ones as a migrant only in winter and summer respectively. He is omnivorous, like other ducks, but has the credit of being an exceptionally enterprising and energetic feeder, and also of being as good as any to eat. He is, as most people know, the ancestor of our tame breeds of ducks, with the exception of the Muscovy, and was domesticated comparatively late, since a Roman writer at about the beginning of the Christian era recommends that ducks be kept in enclosures, netted overhead, lest they fly away, and that the stock be augmented by taking the eggs of wild birds and setting them under hens — so that ducks then were apparently no more tame than pheasants now.

The wild duck, however, is very easily domesticated, and, indeed, degenerates as an ornamental bird in a few generations, becoming heavier and less neatly marked, coarser in the feet, and shorter in the wing; so that for purposes of ornament it is best to get undoubtedly wild birds to start with, and renew the stock when they show symptoms of deteriorating. And few ducks are more handsome than your true Mallard; moreover, he is a good-natured bird with others — rather too much so, in fact, for though, like other ducks, naturally monogamous, he is apt to become a regular Turk when tamed, so that it is as well to allow him more than one mate. It is a curious thing that in its hybrids the Mallard seems very prepotent where colour is concerned, although the other parent gives the shape. I have seen this in crosses with such distinct species as the Pintail, Wigeon, Muscovy, Sheldrake, and Red-crested Pochard. Of domestic breeds of the Mallard only three demand mention in this connection: the grey and white Call Ducks and the so-called East Indian.

## CALL DUCK

### *(Anas boscas var)*

These should be as small as possible, with a short broad bill and rounded forehead or stop. There are two varieties, white, which should have a yellow bill, and grey, which is like the Rouen in colour, *i.e.* closely resembling the Mallard. I have never, however, seen the grey Call Duck, and do not know whether the female should be dark brown in colouring like the Rouen duck, which is darker than the wild colour. Call Ducks used formerly, at all events, to be esteemed for the loquacity of the females, which was useful in enticing the wild birds to the decoys, hence the name. The drake, however, has a weak quack like the Mallard, which, as everyone knows, has a very poor voice compared to his mate. There is not much point in Call Ducks, so far as I can see nowadays, when we have the many beautiful birds I am dealing with in the present series more or less in domestication, with many more nearly or quite untried. It should be mentioned that they can fly like wild birds.

## EAST INDIAN DUCK

### *(Anas boscas var)*

This breed, also called Buenos Ayres, though apparently with no reason in either case, resembles the wild bird in form and power of flight, but should be smaller, in fact as small as possible, even down to two pounds. The plumage is black with a splendid gloss of green and purple, looking as if the drake's metallic hues on neck and wing had spread all over the body. The duck, although she should be as glossy as possible, is naturally less so than the drake, and she has a black bill, while his is olive-green; both have black feet. This is undoubtedly a very lovely breed, although apt to show white feathers with age; but I must say that I

53

think it is a pity both it and the Call Ducks were ever invented, as they tend to mongrelise the Mallard, and no doubt to this cause is due the appalling collection of mongrels which disgrace our London park waters. I now proceed to the consideration of the Mallard's near wild ally kept with us.

## THE SPOTTED-BILL DUCK

### *(Anas poecilorhyncha)*

This is the common wild duck of India and Burma, and is not migratory; nevertheless it is found quite hardy in England, and breeds well here. It is a little larger than the Mallard, longer in neck and leg, and shorter in wing; otherwise in voice, figure, and habits it is nearly identical, though more active. It differs, however, strikingly in plumage, and in both sexes being alike, with, as is usual in such cases, no summer change. They resemble the female rather than the male wild duck, although more showy than she is.

The general colour of the plumage may be described as pale drab, mottled with blackish brown, the drab decreasing behind, till the rump and stern become quite black. The wings bear a large brilliant green bar edged with white fore and aft, and surmounted by a long, white splash, the outer webs of the innermost quills being white. The feet are orange-red and the bill is scarlet at the root, black in the middle, and bright yellow at the tip, a very showy marking, which distinguishes its owner at once. The drakes run brighter in bill and feet than the ducks, which are also apt to fade soon after the moult as regards the white wing-streak, which gets clouded over with drab, at any rate in confinement. This is a fault which wants correction by breeders. But I have often found the sexes so alike in this species that one could only distinguish them by the voice, which, curiously enough, differs sexually just as in the Mallard, although the plumage does not. The Spotted-Bill is a comparatively late introduction, and breeds when in England late in the year, from June to September. It is much inclined to hybridise with the Mallard, and the hybrid is at least partly fertile, so that care is needed to keep the stocks of these beautiful species pure, although fertile hybrids are scientifically interesting and less ugly as a rule than crossbreds.

# PINTAILS

The Pintails, of which three species are well known to fanciers, are surface-feeding ducks, of slender form, with long pointed tails. In the Common Pintail the sexes are very different, but in the Chilian and Bahama Pintails they are much alike.

## THE COMMON PINTAIL

### *(Anas acuta)*

The *drake* of this species not only differs in plumage from the duck, but has a much longer tail and long pointed shoulder-plumes. His general colour is a finely-pencilled clear grey above and pure white below, the latter hue extending up the neck to the head, which is dark brown with a lilac gloss on each side behind the eyes; the stern and long-pointed centre-tail feathers are black, and the shoulder-plumes black laced with pale drab, and the wing-bar bronze-green edged with cinnamon in front and white behind. There is a yellow-buff patch on each flank just before the black vent. The *duck* is dark brown, very clearly laced with buff or white, and usually shows no wing-bar, though a bird now in my possession has one. The tail is barred obliquely with the light colour, which easily distinguishes the female Common Pintail from those of other ducks. Both sexes have grey feet and bill, the latter with a black central stripe and dark eyes.

This is the largest of the Pintails, the drake measuring about two feet in length, more or less, according to the development of the long tail feathers, which may exceed nine inches in length. It is found in a wild state throughout most of the Northern Hemisphere, breeding in the north and migrating south in winter, at which season it regularly visits the British Isles, where a few remain to breed.

In confinement the Pintail drake at once attracts attention by his strikingly aristocratic appearance; his white shirt-front, long, reachy neck, and exquisitely pointed tail stamp him as the "fine gentleman" of his tribe. His manners are in keeping, quiet and inoffensive, and his voice low and unobtrusive. His mate also shares his refined appearance, but her quack is painfully harsh and coarse. Fortunately she speaks but seldom, or her husband might be more ashamed of her than he is. It has been noticed that in a wild state Pintails are particularly given to forming *bachelor* parties! When courting, the Pintail drake suddenly raises himself upright in the water and brings his bill close to his breast, frequently afterwards throwing up his tail in its turn. The species have frequently bred in captivity, and both in this condition and at large has produced hybrids with the Mallard and its descendant, the common tame duck. These hybrids are very handsome, and those between the Pintail and domestic duck have bred again either with the Pintail or between themselves, though in the latter case the ducklings which were bred from the hybrid pair proved to be barren when they grew up. Possibly their parents were too closely related, in addition to their hybrid origin. When the offspring of a Pintail drake and a hybrid duck were crossed with the Pintail, it was found that the taint of the common duck was completely removed. In one case a female domesticated wild duck actually deserted her own Mallard on a Pintail drake being put on the pond, and ultimately paired and produced hybrids with him, a fact that may help to explain the frequency of this cross in a wild state.

The Pintail may be expected to breed in April; the eggs are seven to ten, dull green or greenish buff, and the ducklings are brown above and white beneath. After breeding, the drake goes into undress, and then much resembles the duck, except that he retains the bright wing-bar, and that the light markings of his plumage are white, and partake more of the character of pencilling. Some males undergo this change much later than others, and one confined in a dealer's hutch has been known not to change at all, doubtless he "stuck in the moult" owing to ill-health.

No collection of ducks can be considered complete without this Pintail, and being a European bird it is cheap.

## THE CHILIAN PINTAIL

### (Anas spinicauda)

This very popular duck closely resembles the female of the Common Pintail above described, but the plumage is more of a fawn tint, especially on the head, where it is rusty red; the beak also is bluish only at the tip, the rest being bright yellow, with a black stripe, as in the other species; the wing-bar is dark green, edged with cream colour. This species is considerably smaller than the Common Pintail, the drake being only about twenty inches long, and the duck less, having a shorter tail; she is also not quite so bright, but, on the whole, bears a very close resemblance to her mate. The profile of the bill in this Pintail is very markedly concave or "dished", and its head is certainly not so pretty as the Common Pintail's.

The Chilian Pintail's native country is South America, from Southern Brazil and Peru to the Falklands. It is, however, well established in Europe as an ornamental bird, and breeds freely in captivity; it also often appears at the shows in the Ornamental Waterfowl class. Nature has provided a whole group of Bantam ducks in the shape of the many kinds of Teal, and fanciers would do better to aid in the importation of the many as yet untried kinds of these exquisite little birds than to try and dwarf the species already under their care.

The proper place of the Chilian Pintail is, in my opinion, on a large sheet of water among a mixed collection. It is hardly bright enough for a fancy bird, but its habits are interesting, for, though by make and general behaviour, a surface-feeder, it will, at all events when young, freely dive for food like a Pochard, an action I have never seen the Common Pintail perform. In St. James's Park, where the clear water is admirably suited for observation of the habits of the fowl, I once saw "flappers" diving and catching fish like Cormorants! Here is a fine opportunity for any enterprising fancier who wants to do a little evolution on his own account. The Chilian Pintail seems to have the ordinary habits of a surface-feeder in its wild state, even feeding on dry land at some distance from water, a thing no diving duck would dream of doing. Yet it evidently readily takes to diving, and a course of breeding for this point would probably result in some slight change of form highly interesting to the naturalists. Besides, most people find diving-ducks far more interesting than surface-feeders, and they can naturally forage very much better.

The Chilian Pintail lays in April and August, and sits about a month, twenty-nine or twenty-eight days. The eggs are very pale reddish drab, the clutch containing about nine; the ducklings are dark grey-brown above, paler below, and are very easily reared, feeding readily on dry oatmeal, barleymeal, and breadcrumbs, scattered on water in a shallow pan let into the ground.

Several years ago I exhibited to the London Zoological Society the skin of a curious hybrid between this species and a Carolina duck. The father was a Chilian Pintail which has been flying about the gardens unpinioned, and the rest of the brood, I understood, were pure. The hybrid was more or less intermediate between the two species, but, as often happens, in some points resembled neither parent.

## THE BAHAMA PINTAIL

### *(Anas bahamensis)*

The smallest of the three Pintails I have mentioned, this species is, in my opinion, the most delicately beautiful of all. The drake is nineteen inches long, and his plumage is of a delicate cinnamon, spotted with black below; the shoulder feathers are black, laced with cinnamon, and tail and vent pure cinnamon with no darker markings at all; the wing-bar is metallic green and narrow, broadly bordered with cinnamon; the throat and cheeks are pure white. The feet and bill are lead-colour, with a triangular rose-red patch at the root of the latter on each side.

The female is very like the male, but smaller, with less bright pink on the bill, and plumage duller generally; also she has the eye brown, whereas the eyes of the drake are "vermillion-yellow" or red-chestnut.

This Pintail inhabits some of the West Indies, and most of South America down to the Falklands. It breeds well in Europe, and is frequently shown. Few ducks are more exquisitely coloured than this, and it has the great advantage of possessing practically the same plumage for both sexes, and, as is usual in such cases, not going into undress.

It breeds twice a year, the season being from May to August and the eggs seven to ten in number, pale brown, the second clutch slightly darker than the first. The ducklings are much like those of the Common Pintail. The sex is difficult to distinguish in the fledged young until the second year, the bill up to this time being reddish brown.

I should strongly advise any intending duck fancier to make an early trial of this species, since it presents the advantages of beauty and prolifancy combined; whether it is pugnacious or not I cannot say personally, and the authority I have so frequently quoted does not allude to this point; but according to my own observations and experience Pintails of the other two species are very inoffensive with other waterfowl, so that the pretty Bahama is probably the same, and "a perfect duck" all round.

TUFTED DUCK

# CHAPTER 10

## GADWALL, WIGEONS, AND SHOVELLERS

### THE GADWALL

*(Anas streperus)*

This is a near relative of the Mallard, but rather smaller and decidedly slighter and more delicate in build; it resembles that bird also in habits and distribution, being one of our breeding ducks. However, I only mention it here to warn people against it, unless they are making a general collection of British ducks, for, although a good sporting species, it is not worth its keep as a fancy bird, owing to its dull, uninteresting plumage. The drake is pencilled grey of a dingy tone, with black rump and stern, and the wing provided with a deep cinnamon patch and a white bar, which will at once distinguish him from any surface-feeding duck; the duck is much like the common wild duck, but the white wing-bar readily distinguishes her.

The Wigeons, on the other hand, are most charming little birds; two out of three known species are available. They are at once recognisable by their small neat blue-grey bills tipped with black, long wings, and sharp tails; they measure about a foot and a half in length, so are considerably smaller than the Mallard. Although more or less omnivorous, they are particularly keen on grass, and graze on land like geese, soon eating up all the grass in any small enclosure in which they may be placed, as may easily be seen in the London Zoo in whatever run the Wigeons are kept. This must be borne in mind in keeping them; as they walk well a good grass run is more to the point in their case than a very big pond. One of the available kinds is a British bird, the other a foreigner; so take the former first.

# THE COMMON WIGEON

## (Anas penelope)

Inhabits the northern parts of the Old World, and is probably spreading to the New, since every now and then it occurs on American coasts. In colour the drake is very handsome, being of a clear delicate pencilled grey generally, with white belly and wing-shoulders, and black stern and tail; the head is rich cinnamon with a cream blaze down the forehead and a metallic green shading behind the eye; the breast is greyish pink, and the wing-bar brilliant metallic green and black. The eyes are dark, the bill French-grey, and the feet grey, as in all Wigeons.

The duck is very plain, being dark brown with slight buff lacing, and a white belly; there is no bar on the wing, but the small blue bill easily distinguishes her from other brown ducks.

The drake in undress bears a general resemblance to her, but his prevailing colour is rich reddish-cinnamon, and he retains the bright wing-bar and white shoulders, or changes the latter to French grey; thus he is still easily recognisable, and a sufficiently handsome bird. Young of both sexes resemble the duck, but the drakes show the green wing-bar.

The Wigeon is one of the commonest migratory ducks in Britain, coming in great numbers every winter; it also breeds in some numbers in Scotland, but rarely in Ireland; in captivity it is not a pure breeder, but this matters less as it can be easily and cheaply procured. Apart from the beauty of the drake's plumage, his clear whistling note "whee-ew" makes him attractive, though his dull mate only emits a purring growl.

It has produced Mules with the Pintail and common duck, and also with its near ally, next to be noticed.

# THE CHILOË (CHILIAN) WIGEON

## (Mareca sibilatrix)

This is an inhabitant of southern South America, introduced early in last century. In size, general build, and colour of bill, feet, wings, and belly it resembles the male of the common species, but otherwise its appearance is very different; the head is glossy dark green, with the face white; the breast barred black and white, the back laced with white; the flanks and stern are cinnamon, and the rump black, with a white bar at the root of the tail, which is also black. Drake and duck are alike, except that the latter is not quite so bright, and of course there is no summer change in plumage.

Although lacking the exquisite delicacy of the plumage of the common wigeon drake in full colour, the South American bird is striking, and has the great advantage above mentioned of not varying according to sex and season. It is therefore very gratifying that it is a good breeder and hardy. However, it appears to feel cold winds, and to need maize and animal food in winter. But, of course, all ducks should have shelter from cutting winds, and a certain amount of worms, snails, or other natural animal diet constantly supplied, as, though they can subsist without this, they naturally like a change, being amongst the most omnivorous of birds.

The male of this species utters a whistle; no doubt the female's note is different, as in the common bird. It lays from May to July, the eggs being seven to nine in number. The Mules with the common wigeon I alluded to above, were seen by me some years ago in the London Zoo; they greatly favoured the Chiloë, and, indeed, showed little of the other. It appears that this species has also bred with the Chilian Pintail. Being peaceable as well as constantly showy, it may be safely called one of the most desirable ducks.

## THE SHOVELLER

### (Spatula clypeata)

The Shoveller, although, with the exception of the common Sheldrake, he is about the showiest duck in the Fancy, is, I fear, not sufficiently attractive in personal appearance ever to come into the front rank, by reason of his great ugly bill, broadened out at the top till it is semi-spoonlike in shape, and with the ordinary ridging of the sides developed into a deep horny fringe like whalebone in miniature. Otherwise he is a delicately made bird, with long wings and small feet, and of moderate size, being considerably smaller than the Mallard.

The drake is, indeed, a most brilliant creature, with his big head of a rich metallic green, set off by a golden eye, pure white breast, and cinnamon-red flanks and belly separated from the green-black rump and stern by a white patch; when the wings are opened fresh colours are displayed, the "shoulders" being light blue, and the bar vivid metallic green, while the *tout ensemble* is completed by bright orange feet, the unfortunate bill being plain black!

The duck is much like the common wild duck in colour, but redder below, and her wings are a feeble edition of her own drake's; the bill also differs from his, being olive above and orange underneath, and her eyes are brown; so, on the whole, she has nothing to redeem her "prominent feature".

The drake in undress bears a general resemblance to her, but is darker and redder, and retains his brilliant wings; though his bill assumes the female colour, a rare thing in drakes in undress.

It is a curious fact that Shoveller ducklings are hatched with bills like those of ordinary ducks, though longer and narrower; but the length and breadth have obviously increased at the age of three weeks, especially in drakes.

The Shoveller is another of the ducks which inhabit the northern hemisphere generally, migrating south in winter. Some breed in Britain regularly in the wild state, and it has bred in the London Zoo. A Mule between Shoveller and Garganey has also been kept there, but no result attended the keeping of this bird (a drake) with females of both pure species. The Shoveller, barring its ugly head, is certainly a very ornamental bird on the water, and its habits are interesting. It is the most essentially surface-feeding duck of all I am dealing with, its large, deeply-fringed bill being an exquisitely perfect sifting apparatus, calculated to extract the smallest particles of food from the water; hence it chiefly feeds on the very top, and seldom turns tail-up in the manner so familiar to observers of ordinary surface ducks. It is said to be fond of sifting the water when Pochards are diving below, but I have never seen my own bird — though kept on a large pond in the company of some of these — do this. Probably he gets enough on his own account. At the same time, the Shoveller will eat grain quite readily, and gives no special trouble.

# CHAPTER 11

## TEAL

These birds, the dwarfs of the duck tribe, being only about the size of a large pigeon, resemble nevertheless the ordinary larger ducks in their habits, and, owing to their small size, can easily get a living anywhere where water is to be found, so that it is not surprising that many species of them are found, all over the world.

This smallness makes them very suitable pets for those who can only manage a small pond and enclosure. The former need only be a foot deep and a yard wide for such little birds, and a dozen square yards of enclosure will afford them ample scope. In such a place both our British species, which are the only ones commonly met with in captivity, may be kept; but the enclosure should be netted over completely, as it would be nothing short of cruelty to expose such little birds, if pinioned, in the open, unless a large pond with islands be available for their safe lodgement. Ducks should not, whatever their kind, be confined unpinioned in a **narrow** enclosure, as they cannot, as a rule, turn easily in a small space; and for the same reason newly-acquired birds should have their wings clipped to keep them from injuring themselves when flying at first.

## THE COMMON TEAL

### (Anas crecca)

This is an exquisitely pretty and daintily formed little bird, only about fourteen inches long. The drake is very showy, being of a general pencilled-grey colour, with a breast spotted like a Thrush's and a white belly; the head is rich cinnamon with a broad metallic-green streak, narrowly edged with cream-colour, on each side; the wing-bar is brilliant metallic-green and black, edged with white fore and aft; the stern and a streak down each side of the back are cream and black, and the eyes, feet, and bill all dark.

The duck is dark brown laced with buffy white, and has the wings, eyes, bill and feet as in the drake. He, when in undress, much resembles her, but has the plumage coarsely pencilled with whitish instead of laced.

This Teal inhabits Europe and Northern Asia, migrating south in winter; it visits Britain in large numbers, and also breeds with us, being especially remarkable for the affection it exhibits for its tiny young, which the duck has even been known to follow into captivity. In confinement the Teal breeds well, and is worth taking up with a view to profit, for it is a first-rate little game bird, and no doubt, if a laying strain could be started, eggs from them would be in demand by people wishing to rear the birds for shooting, as is done with wild ducks. And the Teal is a prolific little bird, laying as many as ten to fifteen eggs, which hatch in three weeks; it should be mentioned that several of the smaller ducks take less than the month occupied in hatching by the common duck.

But it is as a pet that I am chiefly recommending the Teal here, and, being so small, it can easily be accommodated in any ordinary aviary of reasonable size, due regard being had to the precautions indicated above. In the large waterfowl aviary at the Calcutta Zoo I have frequently noticed the common Teal perching on the narrow ridges of nesting boxes, though this habit never seemed to be acquired by the next species.

## THE GARGANEY

### *(Querqeudula circia)*

The Garganey is a little larger and coarser in make than the common Teal, and is less brilliantly coloured. The drake has the head and neck pinky-brown finely speckled with white, and set off by a black crown and broad white eyebrows. The breast, rump, and stern are mottled brown and black, much as in the females of many other ducks. The belly is white, and the flanks white sparsely pencilled with black, giving a grey appearance; the shoulders of the wings are French grey, and the wing-bar dull green broadly bordered with white; on each side of the back are some long hackles streaked with French grey, green-black, and

*Figure 11-1* Garganey

white. The eyes are brown, and the bill and feet purplish-grey in both sexes. In plumage the duck resembles the common Teal's duck, but is easily recognisable by having no red wing-bar, or only a very faint reflection of one. The Garganey drake in undress is remarkably like his duck, and can, indeed, be only distinguished by his wings, which still retain their bright colours.

This species of Teal has much the same range as the last, but does not go so far north, and it is much less common in England, where it is known as the Summer Teal. In India, where it is called the Blue-winged Teal, to distinguish it from the other species, it is about the most abundant duck in winter, and in China occurs at times in such numbers that, I have been told, people have actually been alarmed by the roar of the passing flocks at night. In Calcutta I have known a small party spend the day on a tank in the middle of the town, but they were no doubt attracted by a pair of birds which had been there unpinioned the winter before.

As above stated, there are many different kinds of Teal; some are exceedingly pretty, but the only one at all commonly on the market among foreign kinds is the Brazilian Teal *(Nettion brasiliense),* both sexes of which are very similar, and are noticeable for their red feet and beautiful wings of velvety black and metallic-green, the general plumage being brown with a black rump. Another very pretty Teal, which I have seen in the London Zoo, and once in the Calcutta Market, is the East Asiatic Clucking Teal *(Nettion formosum),* of which the drake has the head boldly marked with buff, black, and metallic-green in a manner unlike any other duck's; the rest of his plumage is very pretty, and difficult to describe shortly, but both drake and duck of this species can be recognised by their narrow green and black ving bar, bordered with cinnamon before and white behind.

## THE POCHARDS

The last group to which I shall refer is that of the Pochards, which are diving ducks of heavy form, having broad, squat bodies, short wings, tails and legs, and large heads and feet. Owing to this formation they are awkward and ungraceful on land, and only suitable to be kept where there is plenty of water, in which element they are very active, swimming low, and diving with great agility for food.

Given a good pond, they are very attractive birds; their constant plunging, especially where the water is clear and their motions can be followed, is amusing to watch, and by the same diving faculty they can easily escape from ill-disposed larger companions. Moreover, although the ducks of this section are particularly homely, the drakes have the great advantage of undergoing, as a rule, little or no change in their showy plumage, unlike other ducks. They should have some extra animal food in the shape of snails, worms, small frogs, or fish, etc., and if their grain is given so that they have to dive for it, it will be all the better for them. Five species are commonly to be had, of which the first two I shall mention are considerably larger and less clumsily built than the others. All, however, agree in having a *white or grey wing bar,* and the flights shaded with white or grey, whereby they are easily distinguished from other ducks.

## THE ROSY-BILLED POCHARD

### *(Metopiana peposaca)*

This handsome species, usually known as the **Rosy-billed** Duck, is nearly as big as the common Wild Duck. The drake has a knob at the root of the bill of a bright red colour, the bill itself being pink with a black tip; the plumage is mostly black, glossed with purple on the head, but the flanks and belly are pencilled grey and the stern white. The feet are orange with black webs, and the eye red. He undergoes no 'change in plumage at all after breeding. The duck is brown above and whitish below, with a white throat and stern, and a grey wing bar, the drake's being white. Her bill also is grey, and her eyes brown. The young are much like her, with grey legs. This fine duck inhabits South America, and is a comparatively recent introduction as an ornamental waterfowl, having been imported within the last 100 years. It is a better walker than Pochards in general, and dives less, going under with more of a spring when it does do so. It is a good breeder, and home-bred birds are stated to be superior to wild ones in the colour of the bill and development of the knob at the base — such appendages, indeed, seem to have a tendency to appear or increase in domestication, witness the knob of the Chinese Goose and the wattle of the Muscovy Duck. The breeding time is from July to September.

This is a very showy duck, and the fact that the drake retains his handsome plumage all the year through is a point very much in its favour, both as an ornament and as an exhibition bird, while it needs less water than other Pochards, being content with quite a small pond, as may be seen in the case of those placed back of the refreshment room at the London Zoo, where this species has hybridised with the rest.

## THE RED-CRESTED POCHARD

### *(Netta rufina)*

This is also a large bird for a Pochard, but smaller and squattier than the Rosybill. The head-feathering is very full and soft, especially in the drake, in which it forms a remarkably bushy crest, commonly carried erect, which gives him a very quaint appearance. His colour is also very striking, being light brown above and jet black below and on the rump, with white flanks and a pinky-cinnamon head, the crest being of a lighter shade — a golden-buff, in fact. The white flanks have an exquisite blush of salmon colour when the bird is in fullest colour, and the whole is set off by a scarlet bill and eyes and orange feet with black webs. Taken altogether, he is one of the showiest of all waterfowl.

The duck is a plain light brown and above and greyish-white below from chin to tail; her feet are duller than the drake's, and her bill black with an orange tip. The drake in this species, unlike most Pochards, shows a very marked summer change, and after it resembles the duck very closely, but may be easily distinguished by his red bill and darker belly.

This Pochard inhabits Southern Europe and Central Asia, migrating to India from the latter in winter, when it is very abundant in that country; like the last species, however, it is of comparatively recent introduction as an ornamental bird, and many are still sent to Europe, although it has been bred both on the Continent and in England.

It is a better walker and a less clean and inveterate diver than most Pochards, but still does not look its best on land. However, it is satisfactory to know that it is easily dealt with, for a more striking bird is not easily found, both for the contrasts of its plumage and the exquisite delicacy of some of the hues exhibited, to say nothing of the curious bushy crest. The eggs are also remarkably beautiful, being of a bright green; five to eleven are laid, in the spring. The drake of this species whistles, while the duck croaks like other Pochard ducks, the note of the ducks of this section not being an ordinary quack.

## THE RED-HEADED OR COMMON POCHARD

*(Nyroca ferina)*

This is a very large clumsy-looking duck of medium size, with very large head and feet and broad, flat body. The drake is at once known by his tricoloured plumage, the head being chestnut, the breast and stern black, and the body pencilled grey. The duck has a nut-brown head and breast, and a duller grey body colour. Both have grey and black bills and feet, like all the remaining Pochards. The drake does not go out of colour much, merely becoming duller in summer. His eyes are red, while the duck's are dark brown.

This Pochard has a wide range in the Old World, breeding to the north and migrating south in winter. The American Pochard is hardly more than a variety, but in America is found also the celebrated **Canvas-back** *(Nyroca vallisneria),* which is now popular in Europe; it much resembles this Pochard, but is much larger and lighter below, with the bill all black. The Common Pochard breeds in small numbers in England, but is not a free breeder in confinement, in which state, however, its tameness and striking plumage make amends for its clumsy form. It is a very fine diver, like all those I shall have occasion to mention hereafter, and gets about better on land than one would expect from its build, though it looks most clumsy there.

A bird I had appeared to remember me after an absence of three months, and St. John in his *Natural History and Sport in Morayshire* gives an instance wherein a Pochard, after escaping, recognised its friends and seemed pleased to see them. This Pochard has hybridised in captivity with the Tufted Pochard, the progeny proving fertile with one of the parent stocks. The wild bird known as "Paget's Pochard" is believed to be a hybrid between this species and the next on my list.

# THE WHITE-EYED POCHARD

## (Nyroca africana)

This is the smallest of the Pochards, and a comparatively neat-looking bird, with very tight, sleek plumage; it is about sixteen inches long. The drake's leading hue is a bright mahogany red, with black back and white belly and stern, only the latter showing when on the water, however. The eye is of a pearly whiteness in him, while in the duck it is dark grey. She is also much duller and darker in colour, with the white belly less clearly defined, and is a very dingy, ordinary-looking little duck altogether. The drake, however, makes some amends by never going "out of colour", although some breeders experience appears to contradict mine in this particular; the point is one well worth investigation, for it would be a remarkable thing if some drakes changed and some did not in this species. The young birds are dirty yellowish-brown, with dark brown-and-white wings, as in adults.

The White-eyed Pochard is found in Europe and Western Asia, migrating to Africa and India in winter, and also breeding in Kashmir and North Africa; it is occasionally shot in England, but has never bred there, even in captivity. It is, however, a desirable bird, the drake's colour being very handsome in a good light, and it will thrive even with a small pond, though I do not advise that it should be so treated. It is a remarkably fine diver, and fond of keeping to cover in a wild state, so that a pond provided with plenty of rushes, etc., will suit it well. It has been known to live fifteen years in confinement.

# THE TUFTED POCHARD OR TUFTED DUCK

## (Fuligula fuligula)

The last species I shall have occasion to notice is one of the most attractive of all; round and tubby in form and of small size, being little bigger than the White-eye, the Tufted Drake at once attracts attention by his pied plumage, the belly and flanks being white and the rest of the plumage black, glossed with purple on the head, which is adorned with a long, narrow, drooping crest. The bill is of a peculiarly light clear blue-grey and the eyes golden.

The duck of this species may at once be identified by her short, small crest; her eyes and bill are duller than the drake's, and her plumage is dark brown where his is black, and shaded with brown on the flanks. The drake in undress merely gets a shorter crest and black shading on the sides. The young birds are dirty light brown, much like young White-eyed Pochards, but their crests soon appear, and their yellow eyes also distinguish them early. The Tufted Pochard has a wide range in the Old World, breeding to the north and wintering in the south, like so many other ducks. It visits us regularly every winter, and a good number breed in our islands. It is one of the very best of ducks for a piece of ornamental water, as the plumage of the drake is very showy, and it is an admirable diver, and thus amusing to watch; it is also the best breeder of all the Pochards, and becomes polygamous in domestication, although so peaceable that several pairs may be kept together. The eggs are six to eight in number, large for the size of the bird, and hatch in three weeks. The ducklings dive at once, and I have watched their evolutions in St. James's Park with much interest. They begin to go to nest in April, but may not breed till two years old. In addition to the cross with the common Pochard above mentioned, the Tufted Pochard has crossed in the London Zoo with the White-eye fifty years ago, and for about a dozen years the hybrids continued to breed either with each other or with one of the parents — a nice lot of mongrels they must have been, but the fact is one of great scientific interest nevertheless. However, crosses of this kind are not likely to be encouraged by a fancier who likes a nice looking collection. Pochards are not much for exhibition purposes, as they don't look well out of water, and the tufted species especially is a very clumsy pedestrian; but for pets they are particularly suitable, and this little tasselled bird is, to my mind, the best of the lot.

There are many other ducks of the diving section which may be occasionally obtained, but I have not thought it worth while to mention them, although I hope sooner or later to see them more generally kept. Such are the Golden-eye *(Clangula glaucion),* noticeable for its dark head, small bill, and pied body; the Scaup *(Fuligula marila),* much like the Red-headed Pochard, but with a dark green head instead of red in the drake; the well-known Eider Duck *(Somateria mollissima)* which bred for years in the London Zoo, though I have never seen it there; and the narrow-billed fishing-ducks or Mergansers, whose feeding habits render them unsuitable for fanciers, though their plumage is very handsome, especially in the case of the smallest, the Smew *(Mergus albellus),* the drake of which is nearly all white, and which is fortunately about the easiest to keep. However, the duck Fancy will have to advance considerably before there is much chance of getting other ducks widely accepted than those I have treated of in this brief account. Should it have been the means of awakening anyone's interest in the ducks as fancy birds, I shall deem the trouble of writing it most amply repaid.

*Figure 11-2*   Red Crested Pochard

# APPENDIX

## WATERFOWL INCUBATION PERIOD (IN DAYS)

**SWANS**

Bewick's, 34-38
Black, 34-37
Black-necked, 34-36
Coscoroba, 35
Mute, 35-38
Whooper, 35-42

**GEESE**

Andean, 30
Ashy-headed, 30
Bar-headed, 28-30
Barnacle, 25-28
Bean, 27-30
Brent, 25-28
Canada, 27-30
Cereopsis, 35
Egyptian, 28-30
Emperor, 26-28 (usually 27)
Greylag, 27-30
Lesser White-fronted, 25-28
Magellan, 30
Pink-footed, 25-28
Ruddy-headed, 30
Snow, 24-28
Swan Goose, 30
White-fronted, 28-30

**DUCKS**

Argentine Red Shoveler, 23
Australian Wood, 28
Bahama Pintail, 25
Baikal Teal, 23

Black East Indian, 28
Blue-winged Teal, 23
Brazilian Teal, 25
Buff Orpington, 28
Cape Teal, 25-26
Carolina, 28-30
Chestnut-breasted Teal, 27
Chilean Teal, 25-26
Chiloe Wigeon, 25
Cinnamon Teal, 23
Common Pintail, 23
Common Pochard, 25
Common Shelduck, 28
Common Teal, 23
Decoy Duck, 28
Falcated Teal, 26
Fulvous Whistling Duck, 30-32
Gadwall, 23-24
Garganey, 23
Laysan Teal, 25
Mallard, 28
Mandarin, 28-30
Muscovy, 35
Pochard Red-crested, 25-26
Red-billed Whistling Duck, 27
Rosybill, 25-26
Shelduck Ruddy, 28-29
Scaup, 28
Shelduck South African, 29-30
Shoveler, 23
Spotbill, 26
Tufted, 25-26
White faced Whistling Duck, 28-30
Wigeon, 25

Chapter 12

## FURTHER ILLUSTRATIONS OF WATERFOWL

Further illustrations of waterfowl are given on the pages which follow. All these birds may be kept by the amateur, except, possibly, the Red-Breasted Goose, which is expensive to buy and *may* be difficult to breed, and the Eider Duck. In the author's experience much depends upon the conditions prevailing; this was confirmed when visiting a woman breeder who had great success with Red-Breasted Geese which she attributed to a large lawn and a wide, slow flowing river.

The *coloured* plates (in a separate section) should be studied with care. They indicate the shape and feather colour and conformation of typical species. When you visit the Wild Fowl Trust at Slimbridge or Arundel, or in other areas, look carefully and try to recognize each of the species. Taking a Note Book and camera will add to the interest, allowing a permanent record to be kept for future reference.

*Figure 12.1* Chilian Pintail – a popular species

*Figure 12.2* White Faced Tree Duck

*Figure 12.3* Call Ducks

*Figure 12.4* Muscovy and Duckling — a very hardy species

*Figure 12.5* Mallard Drakes with Duck in Centre

*Figure 12.6* The Smew — easily managed

*Figure 12.7* Canada Geese — very popular but need a large pond

*Figure 12.8* Eider Ducks and Nest (A fascinating species but not usually kept)

*Figure 12.9* Shoveller

80

*Figure 12.10* Red-Breasted Geese. Beautiful Geese, but very expensive and not recommended for the amateur

*Figure 12.11*  Pink-footed Geese

*Figure 12.12*  Grey-lag Goose

# INDEX

**A**
African Ruddy Shelduck     37
Australian Shelduck     37

**B**
Breeding     11
Brooding     12, 13, 14, 17
Broody Hens     12

**C**
Common Shelduck     34

**D**
Diseases     8
Drowning – danger     15
**Ducks**
    Bahama Pintail     58
    Brazilian Teal     67
    Call     53
    Carolina     44
    Chilian Pintail     56
    Choosing     7
    Common Pintail     55
    East Indian     55
    Eider     72
    Fulvous     50
    Gadwall     60
    Garganey     63
    Goldeneye     72
    Mallard     51
    Mandarin     40–43
    Merganser     73
    Muscovy     38
    Pochard     67, 68
    Pintails     55
    Scaup     72
    Red-billed Whistler     48, 49
    Shelducks     33–37
    Shoveller     62
    Small Indian Whistler     48
    Smew     73
    Spotted-Bill Duck     54
    Teal     42, 62
    Treeducks     46–50
    Whistlers     46–50
    White-eye     72

**Ducks** Continued
    Wigeons                         60, 61

**E**
Eggs                                14
Enclosure                      1

**F**
Feeding                         7
Foodstuffs                   8

**G**
**Geese**
    Bar-headed                24
    Barnade                   26
    Bean                       22
    Brent                     27
    Canada                   26
    Cereopsis               28
    Chinese                 24
    Egyptian               31
    Grey-lag               22
    Magellan              29, 30
    Pink-footed            23
    Sebastopol            23
    White-fronted        23

**H**
Hatching                  11
Humidity                 15
Hybrids                  7

**I**
Incubation             12, 15
Incubation Periods      74
Incubators             15

**M**
Moisture                 16

**P**
Pinioning               6
Pochards              67–73
Ponds                   1
    Fibre Glass           4
    Types                2, 3

**R**

| | |
|---|---|
| Rearing | 17 |
| Ruddy Shelduck | 34 |

**S**

| | |
|---|---|
| Showing | 9 |
| Space Required | 9, 10 |
| Swans | |
|    Bewick's | 20, 21 |
|    Black | 19 |
|    Black-necked | 21 |
|    Mute (Tame) | 18, 20 |
|    Whooper | 20, 21 |

**T**

| | |
|---|---|
| Temperatures | 16, 17 |
| Turning (Eggs) | 16 |

**V**

| | |
|---|---|
| Variegated Shelducks | 36 |

**W**

| | |
|---|---|
| Water | 5 |
| Water-supply | 5 |
| Weeds | 5 |